COLORING MANDALAS FOR ADULTS AND CHILDREN

The Ultimate Antistress Book

Lumina Visions

The pictures contained in this book have been generated
by copyright-free Ai generator

AI and humans are not perfect. All the images contained
in this book have been checked by humans and they
resulted copyright-free. Despite that, machines are not
perfect: if any of these mandalas are protected by
copyright and you want them removed, just contact us!

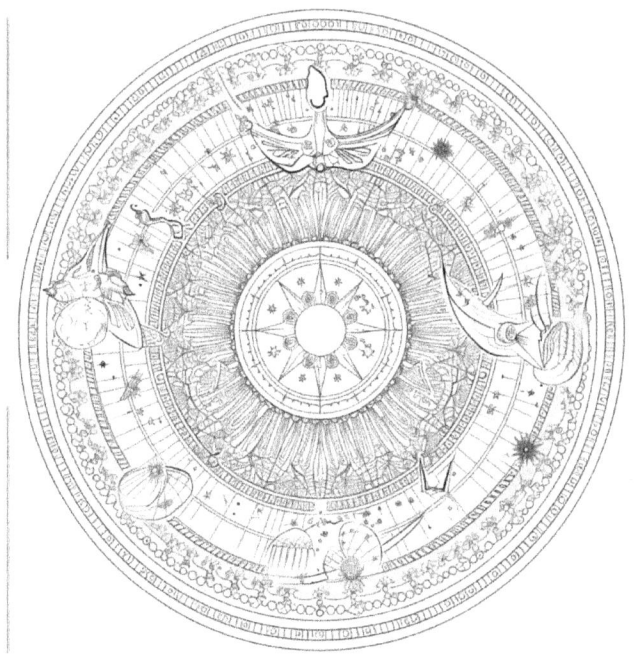

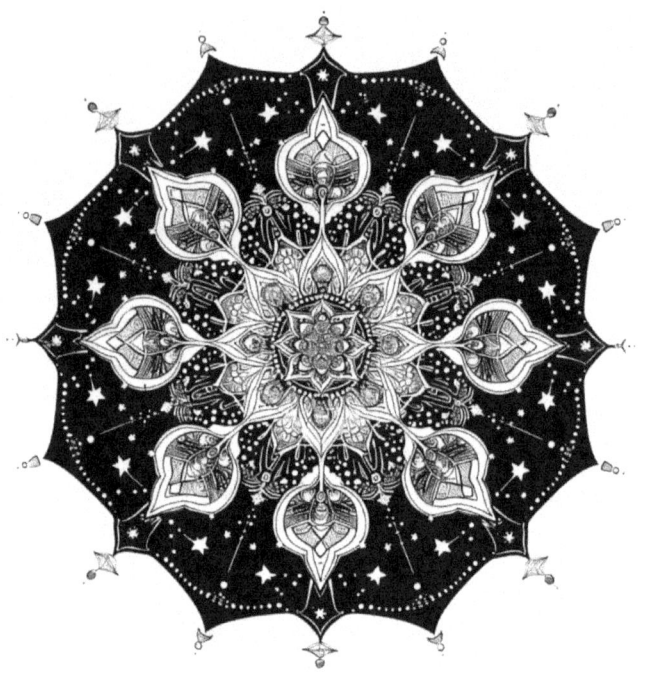

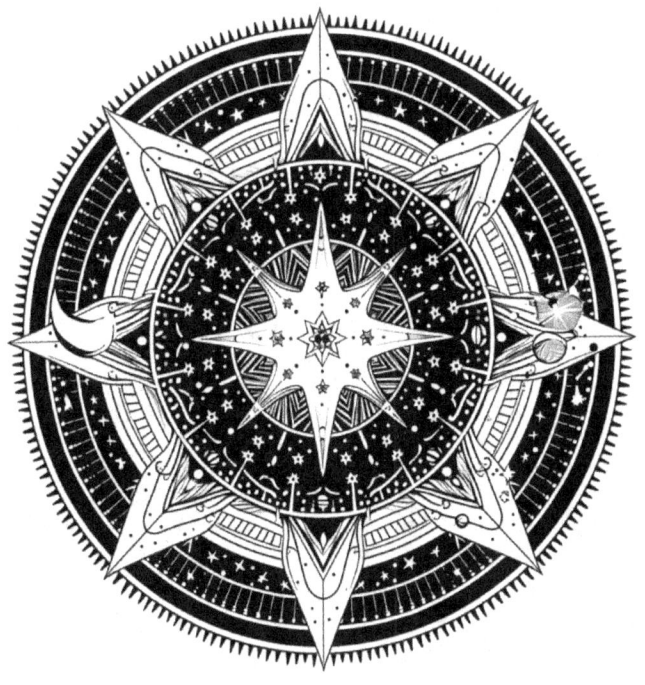

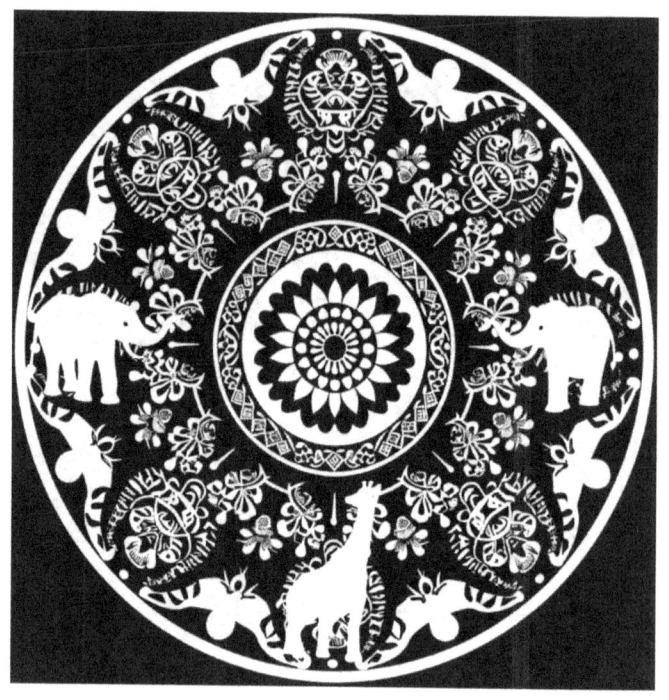

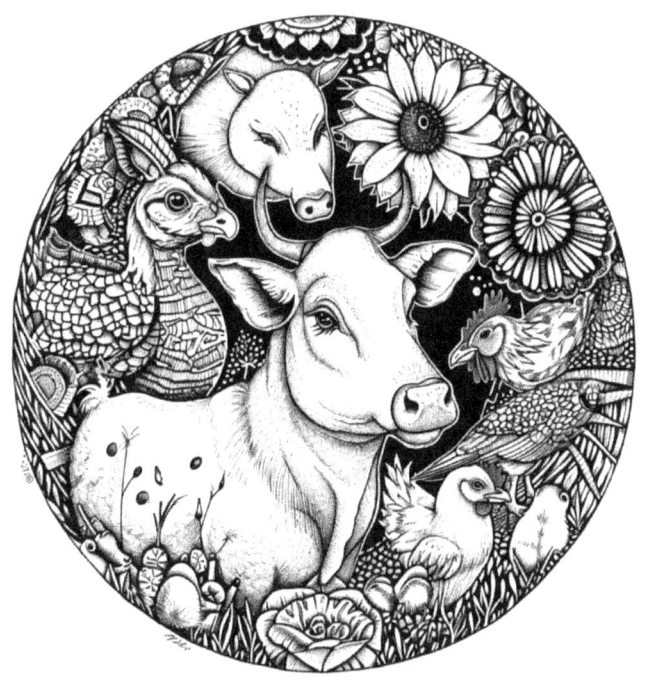

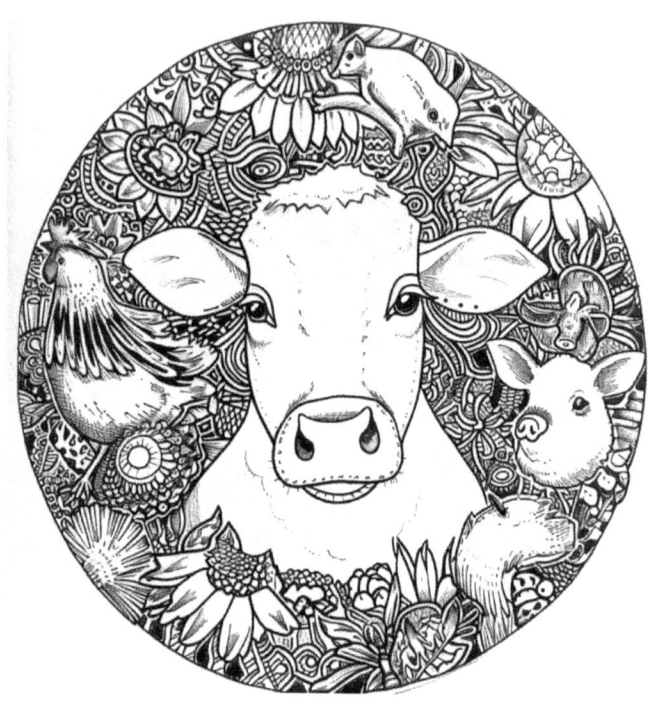

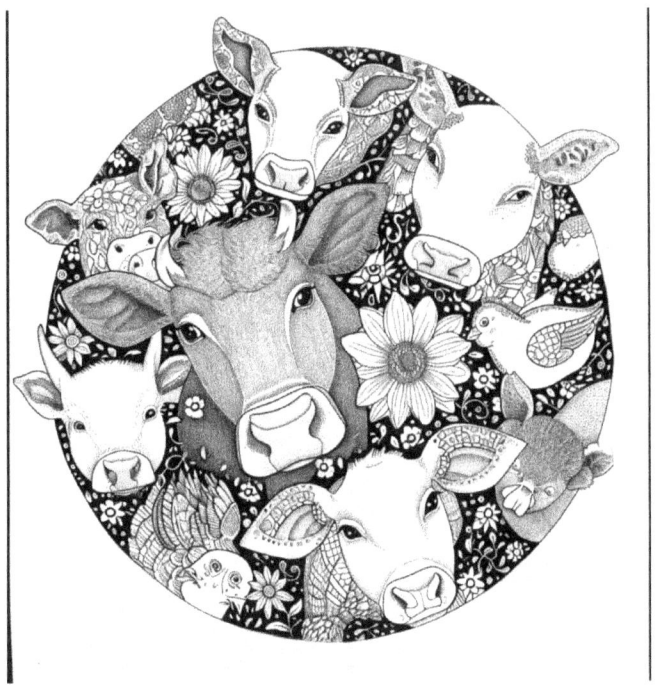

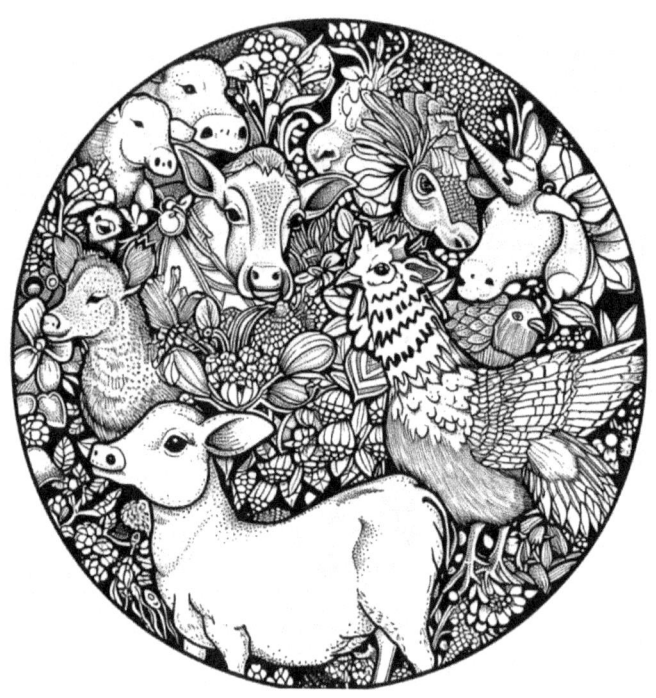

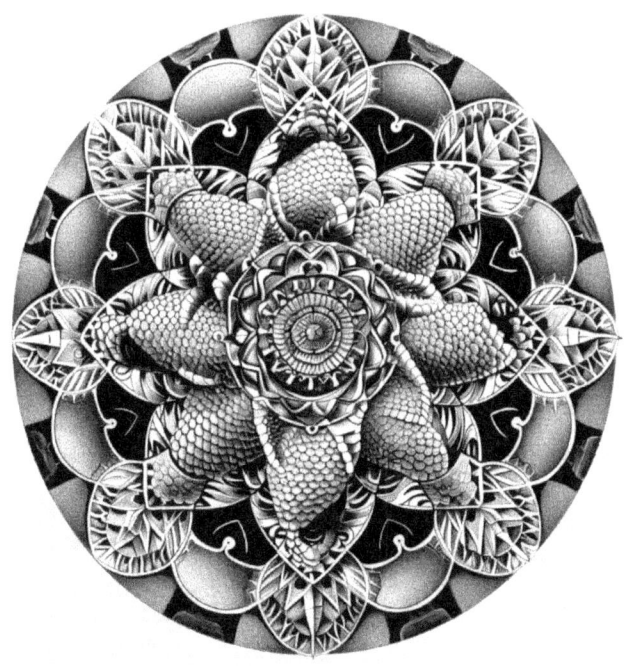

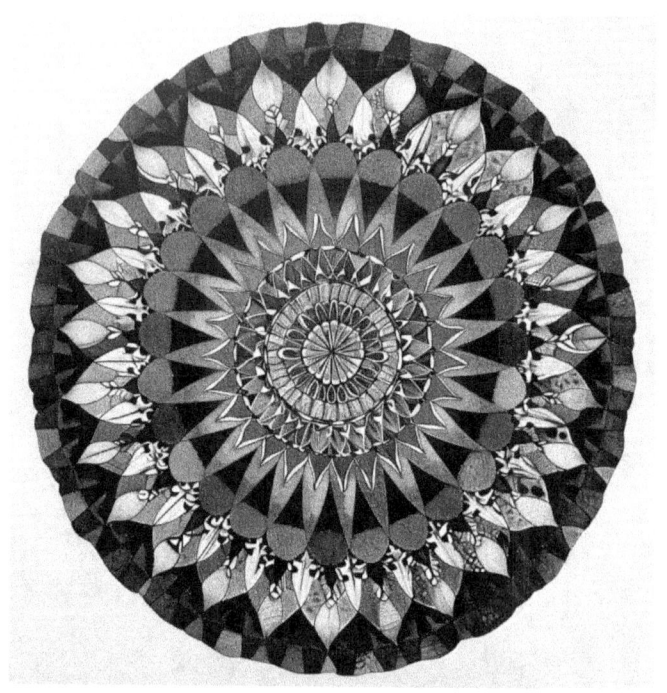

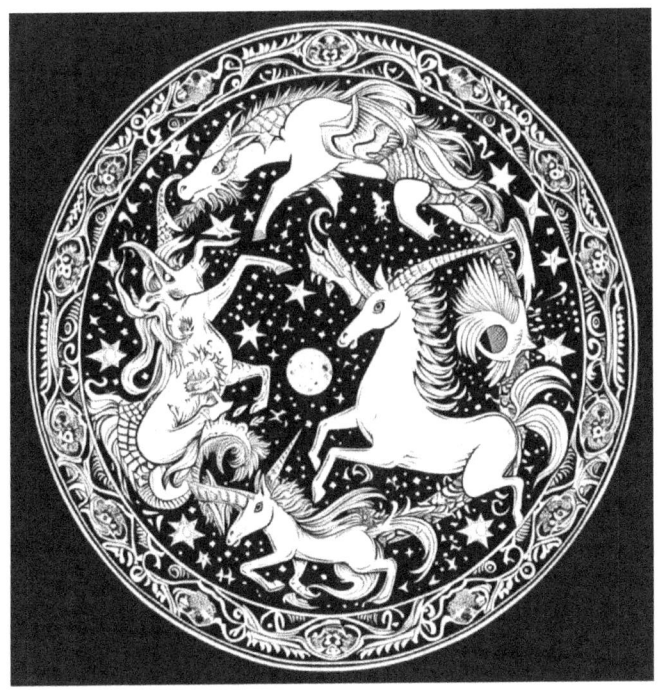

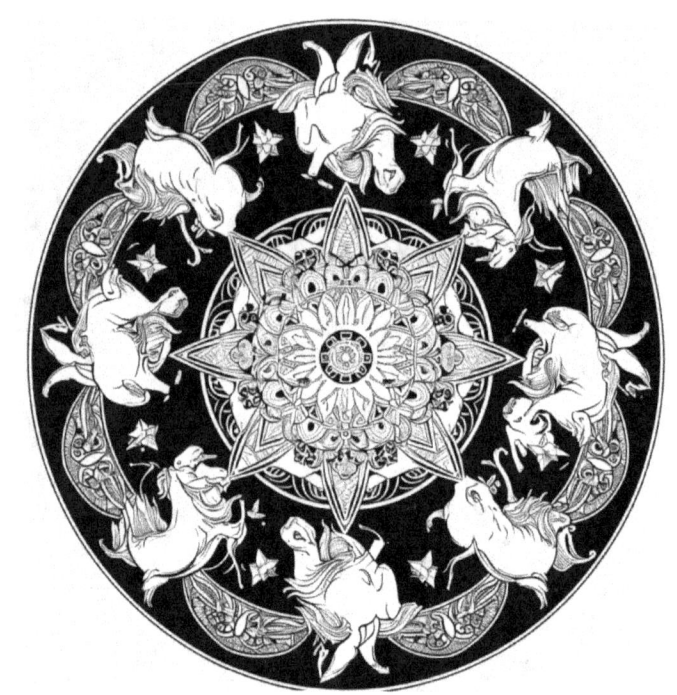

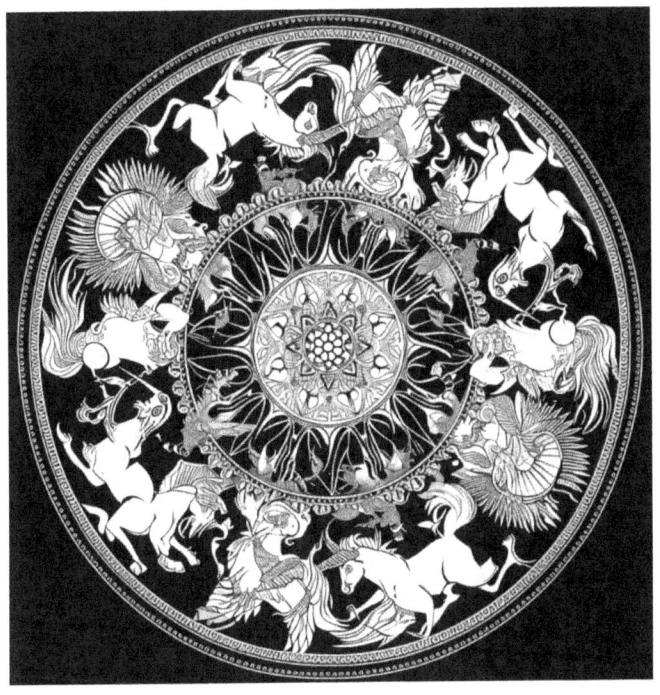

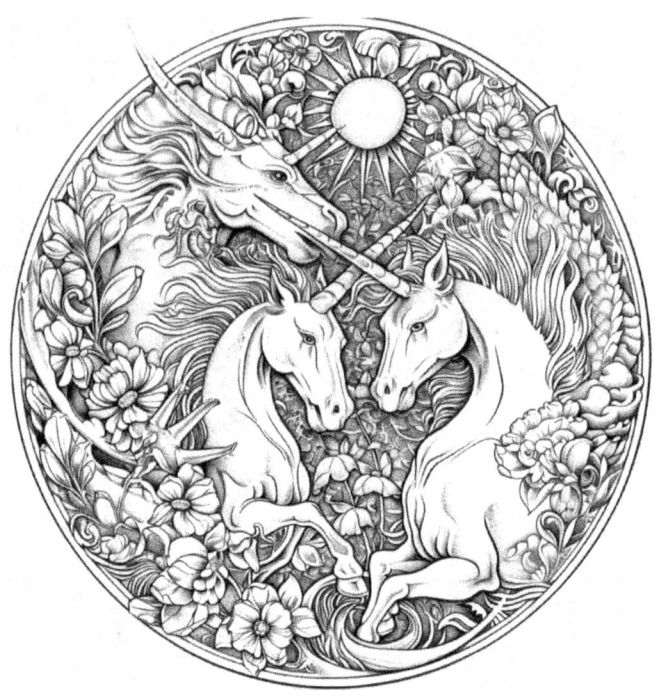

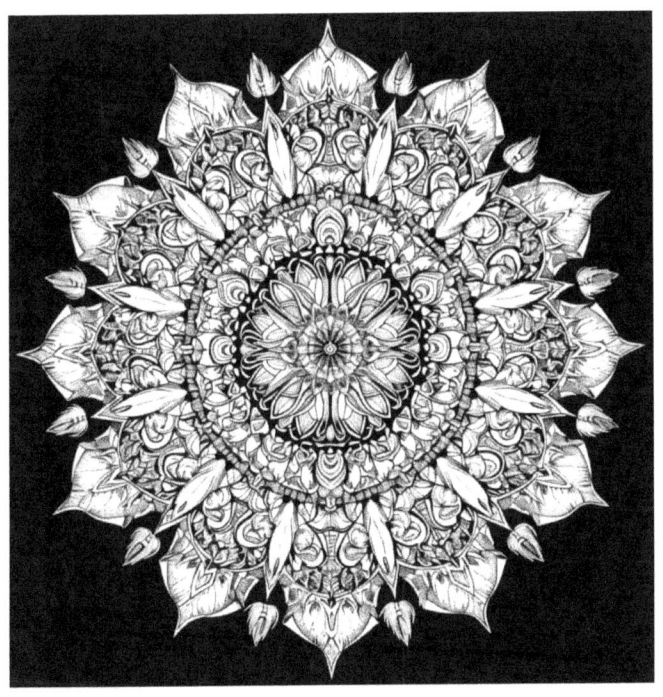

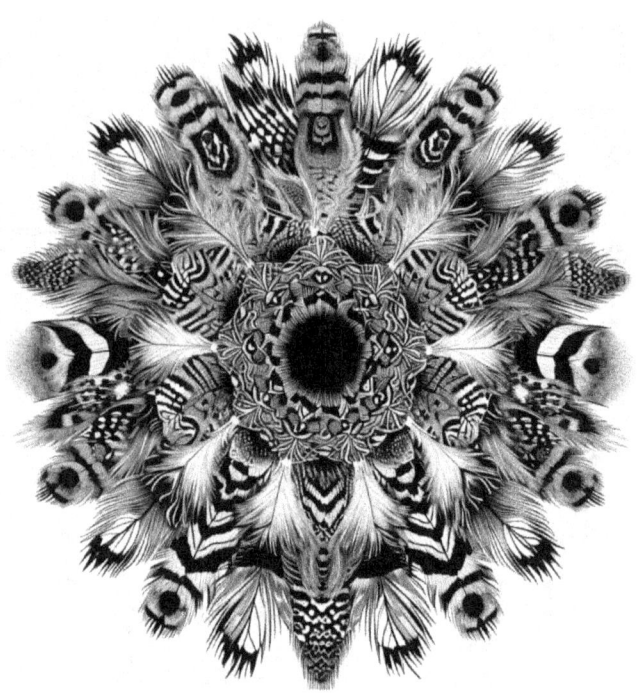

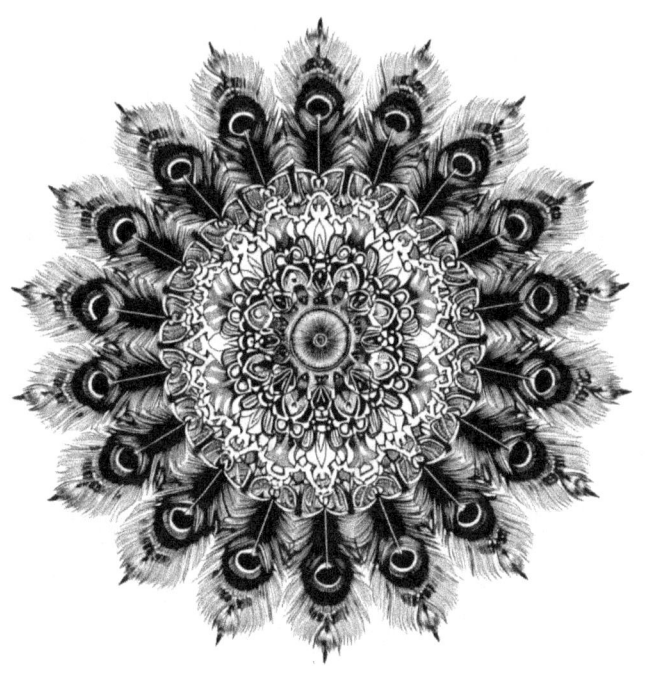

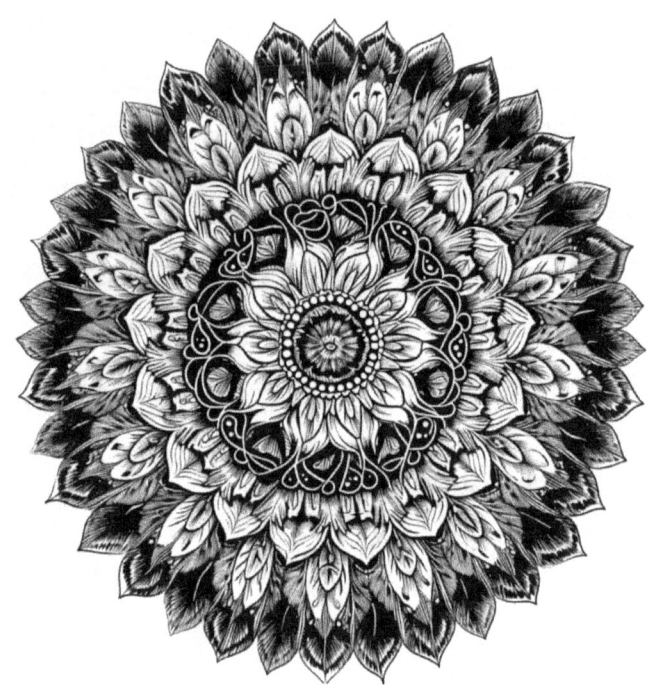

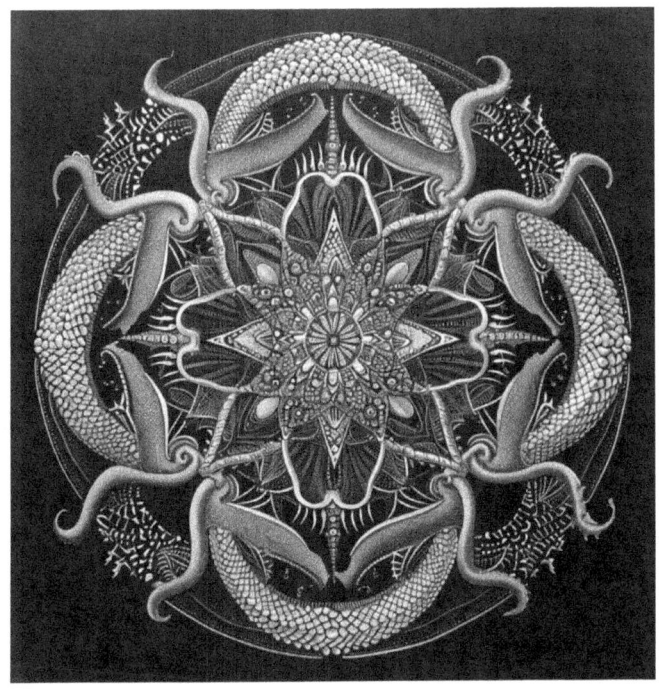

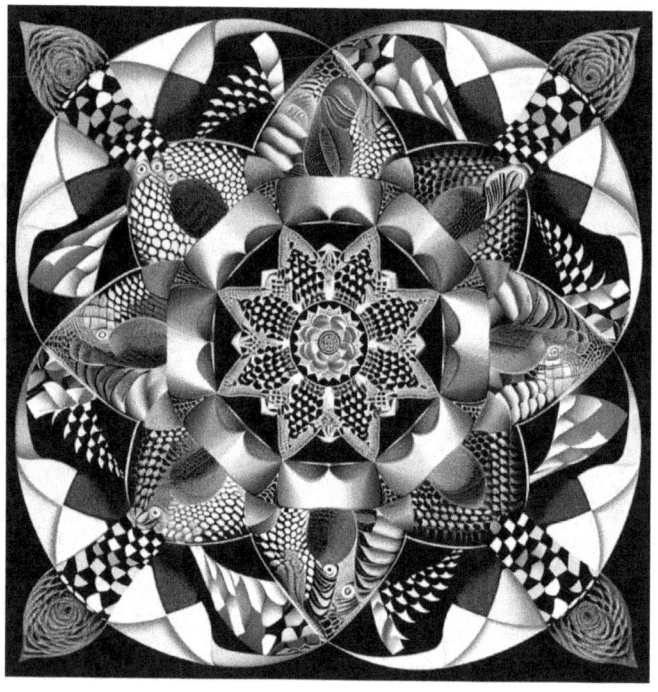

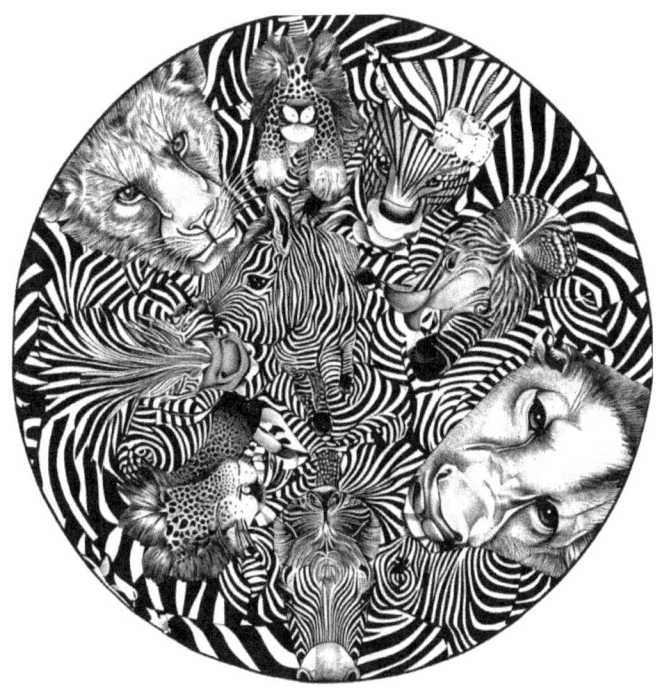

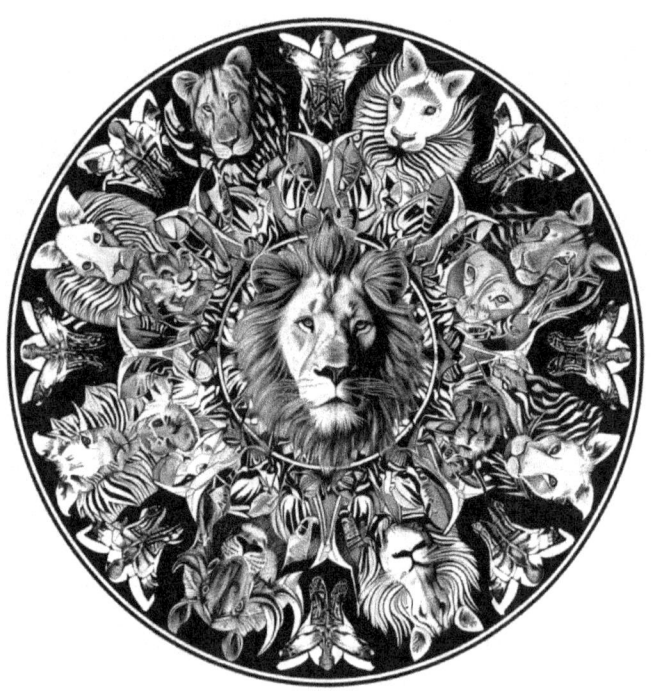

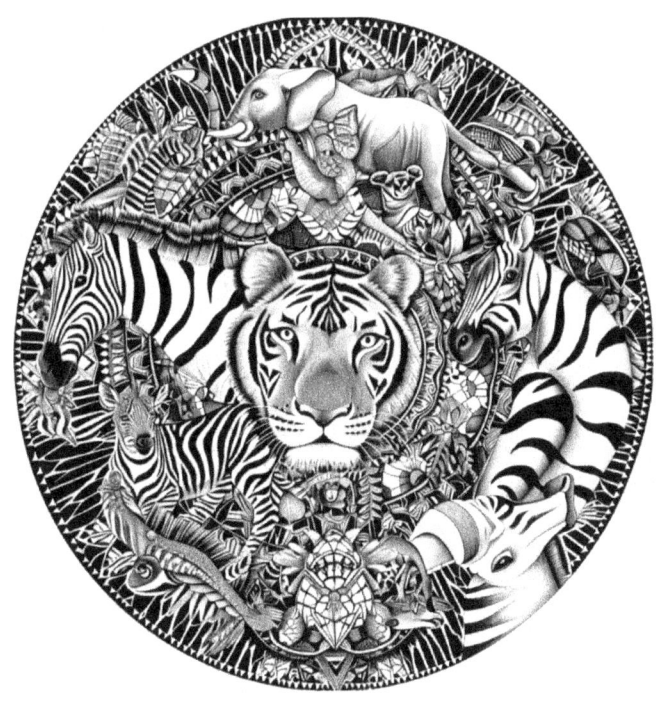

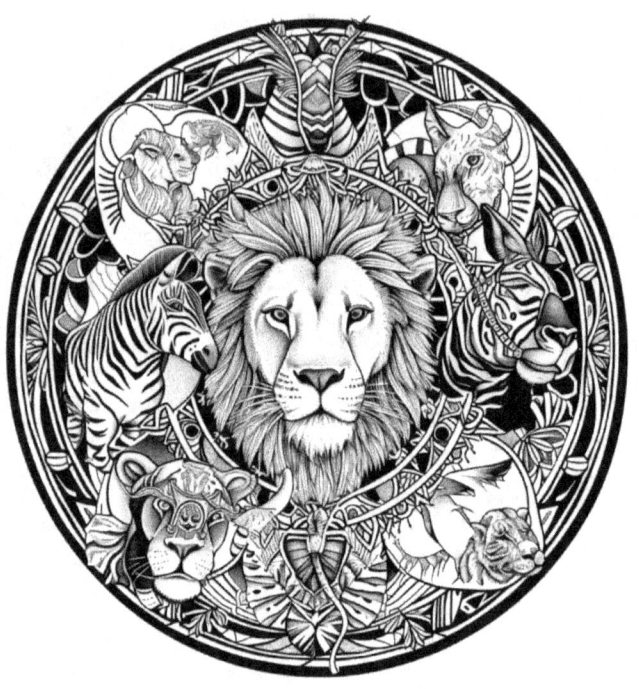

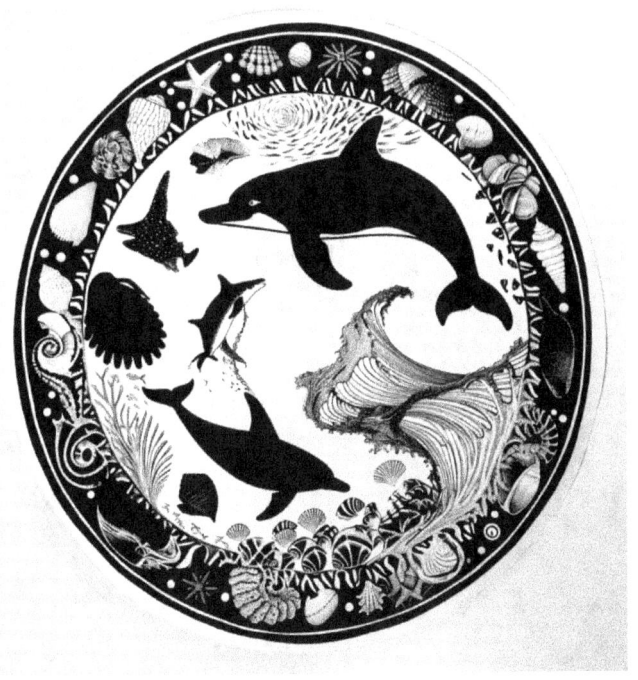

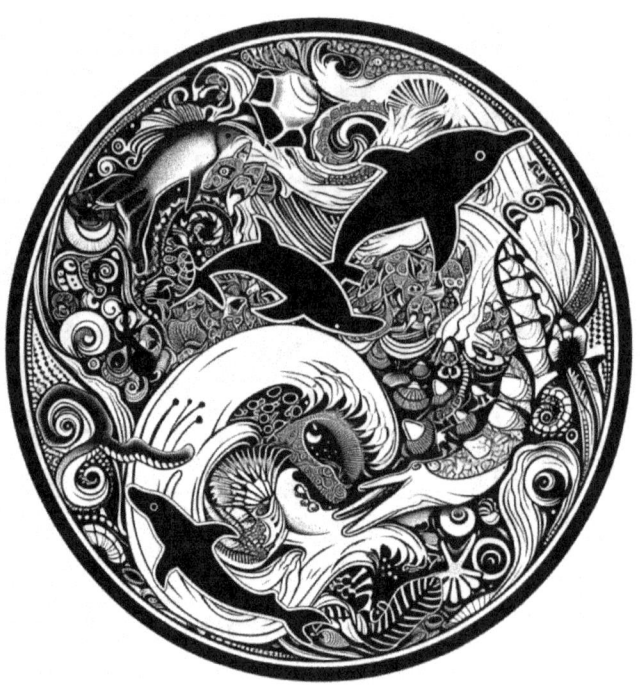

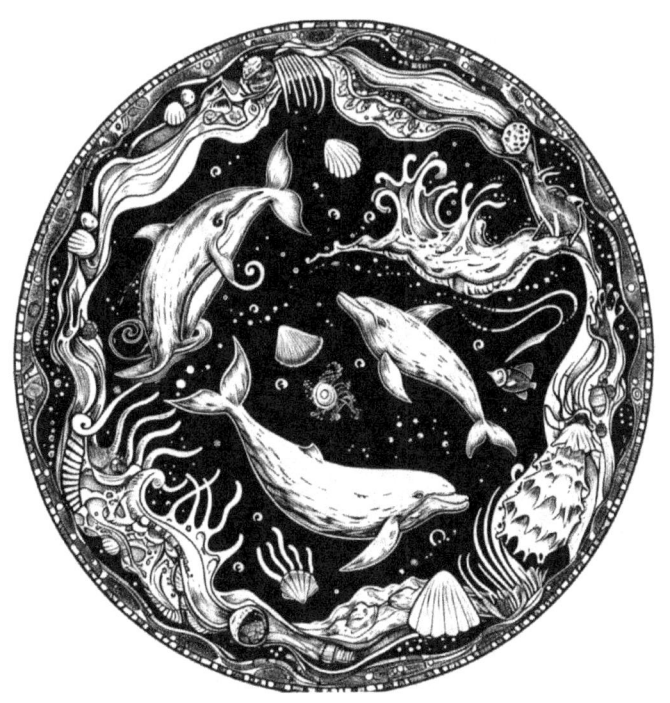

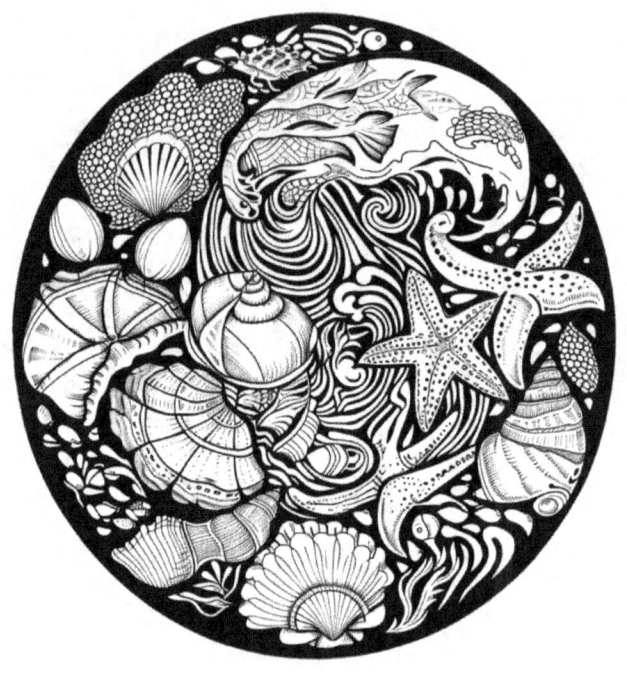

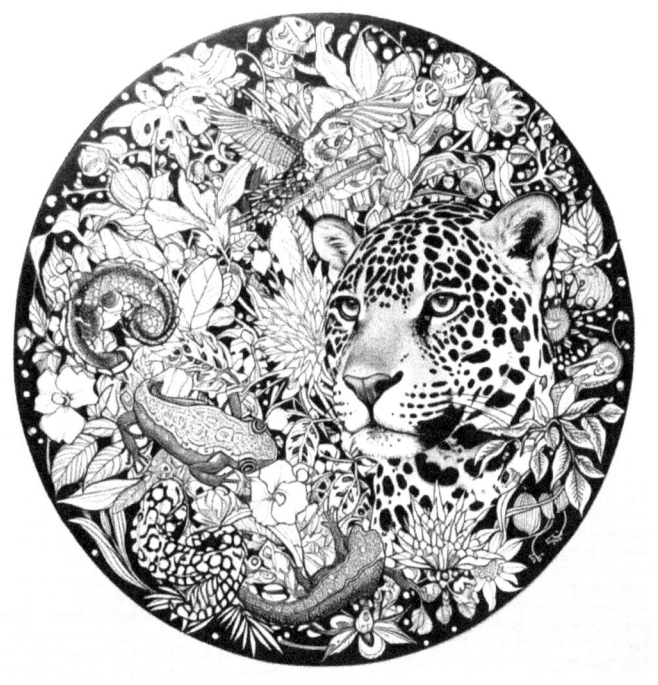

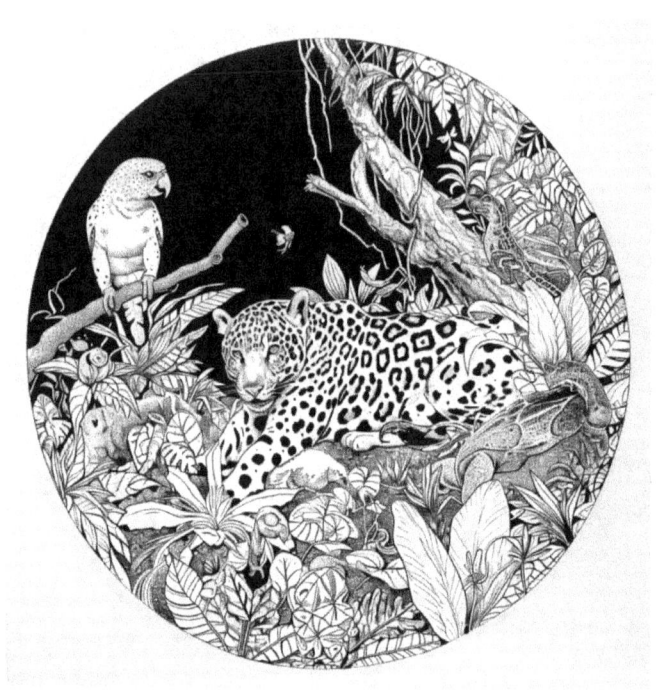

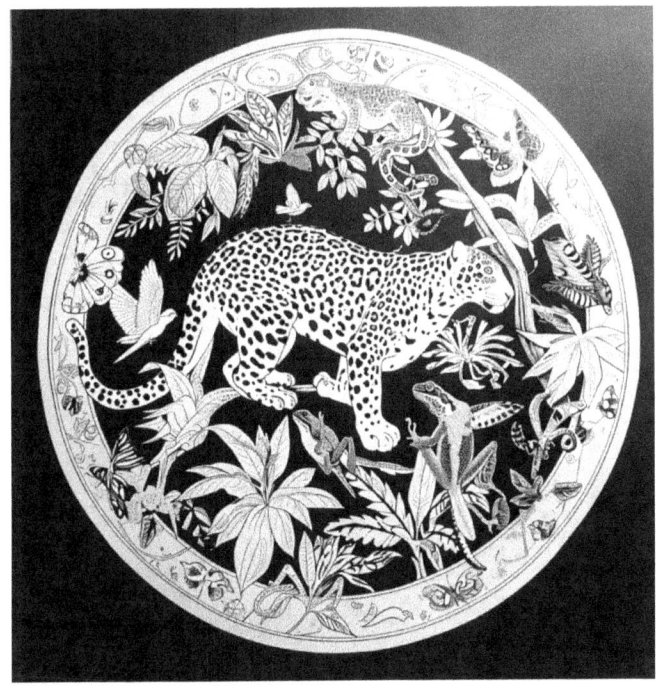

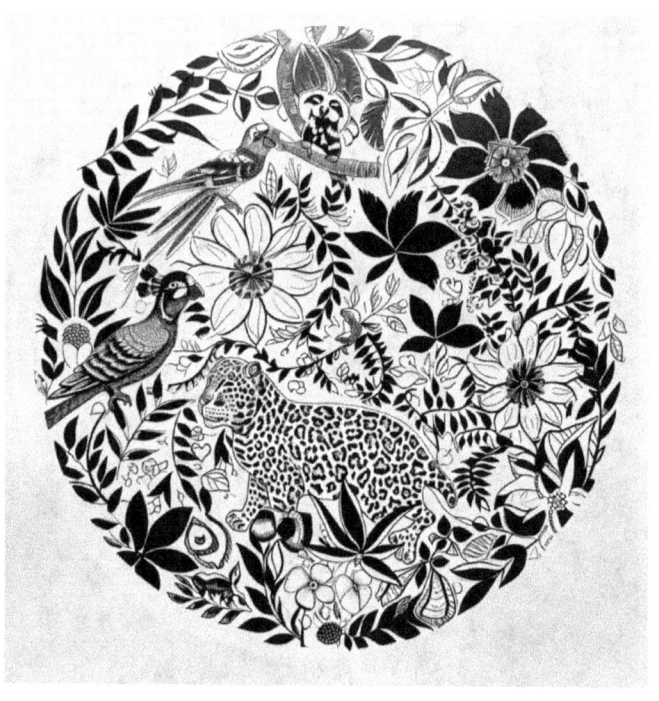

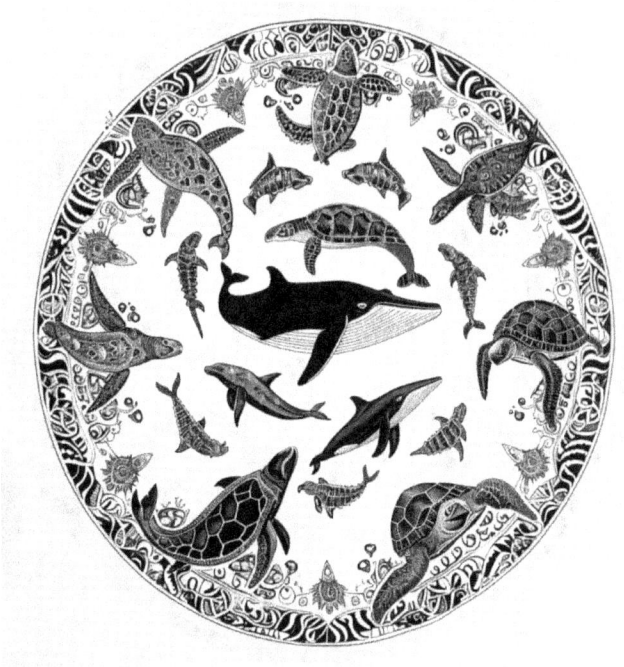

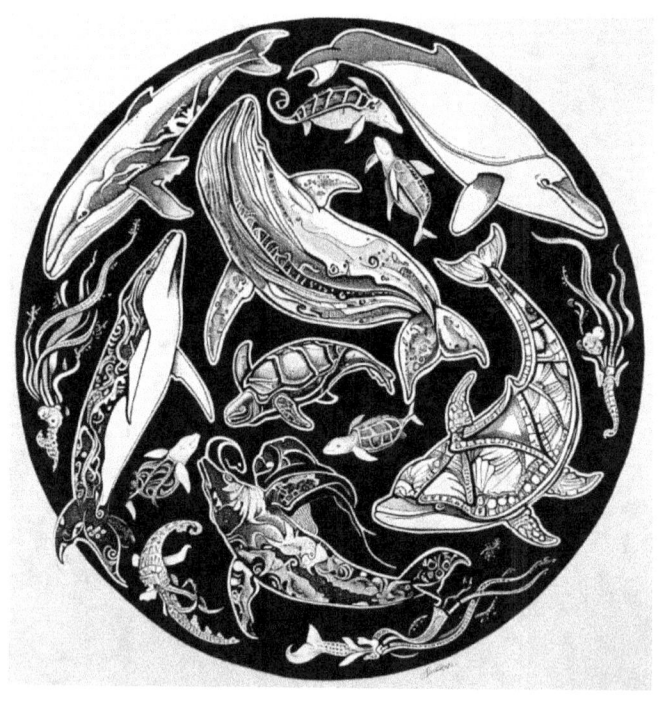

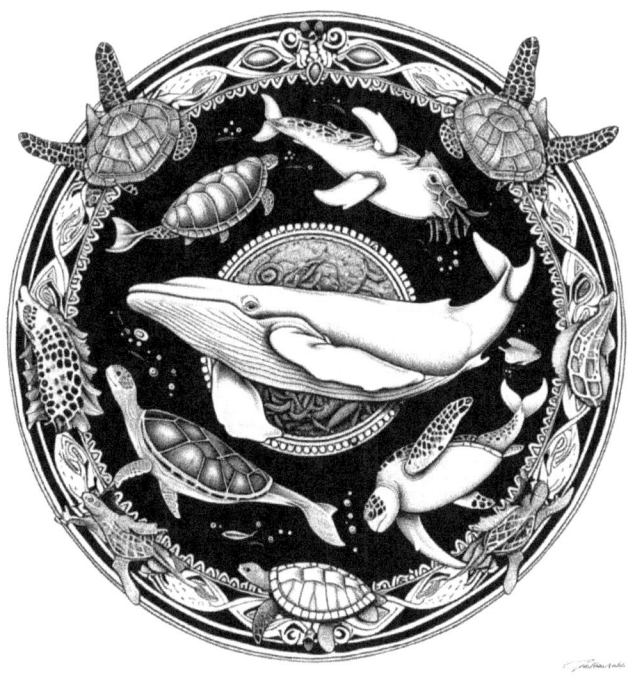

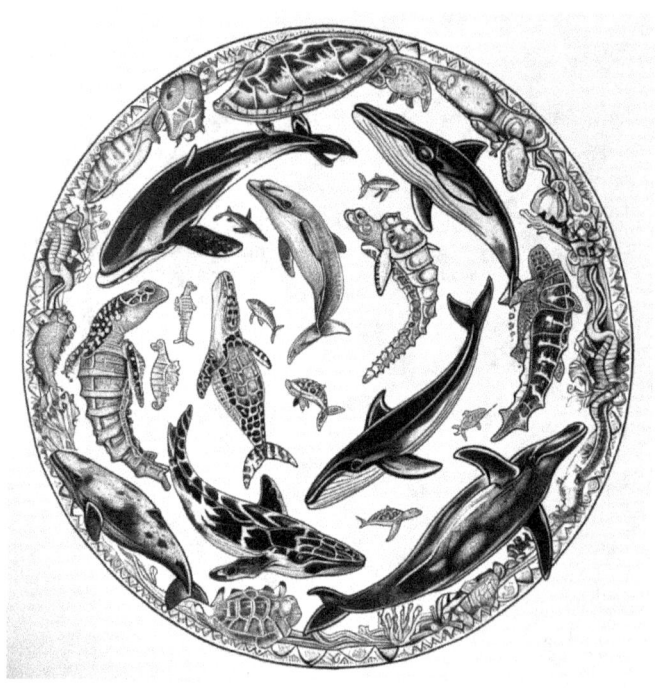

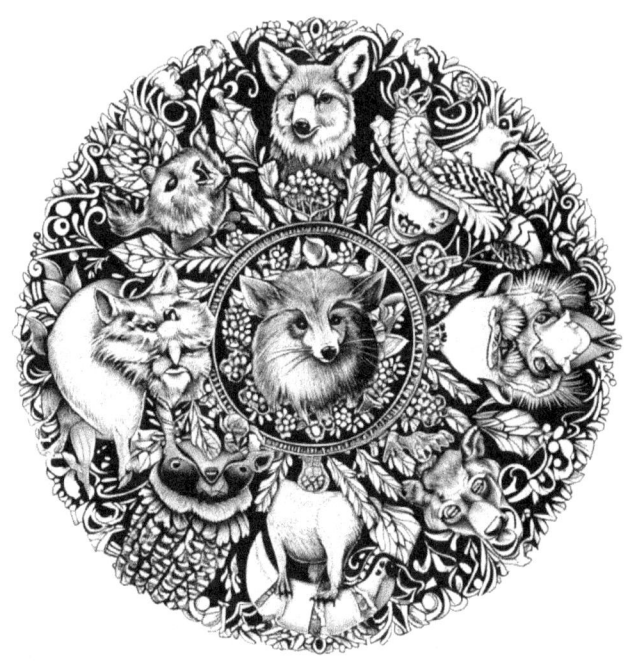

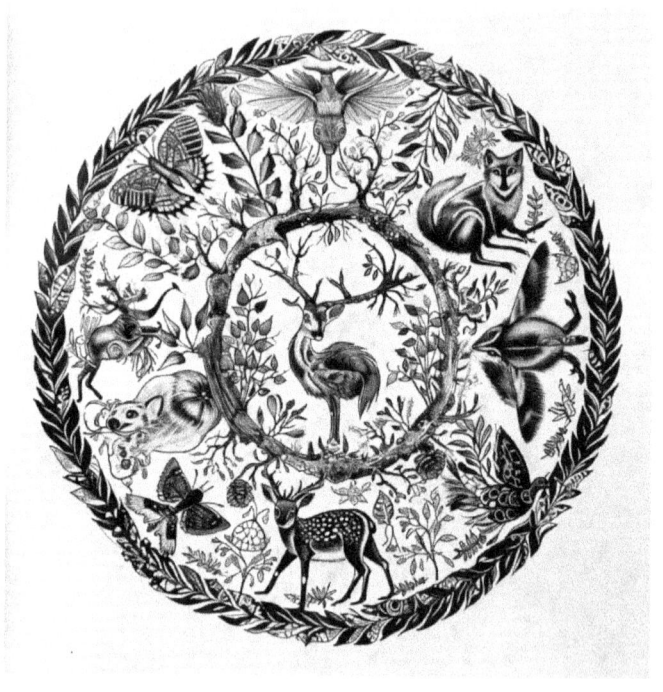

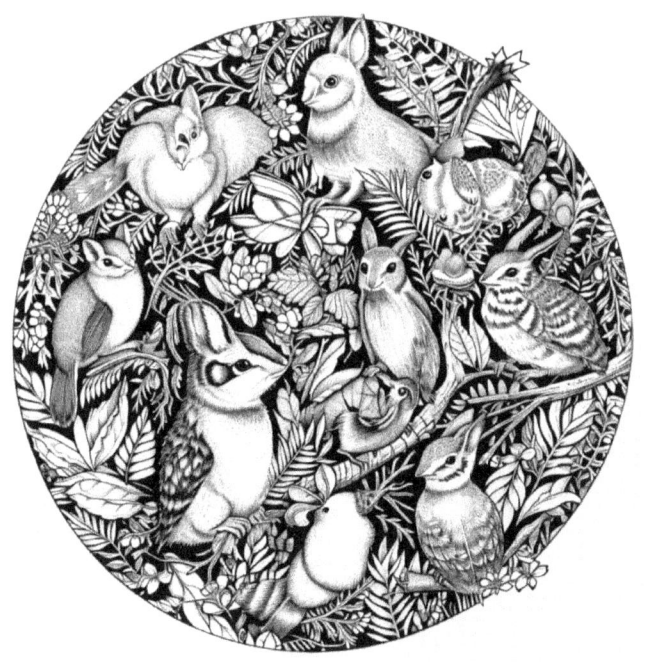

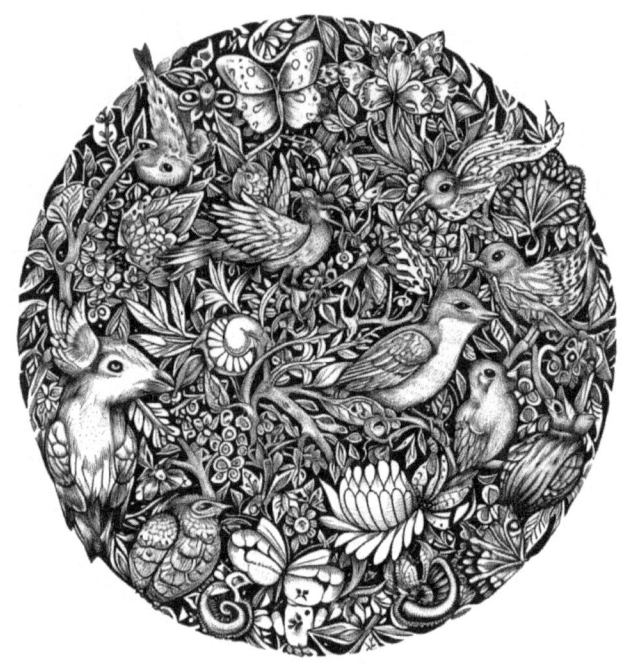

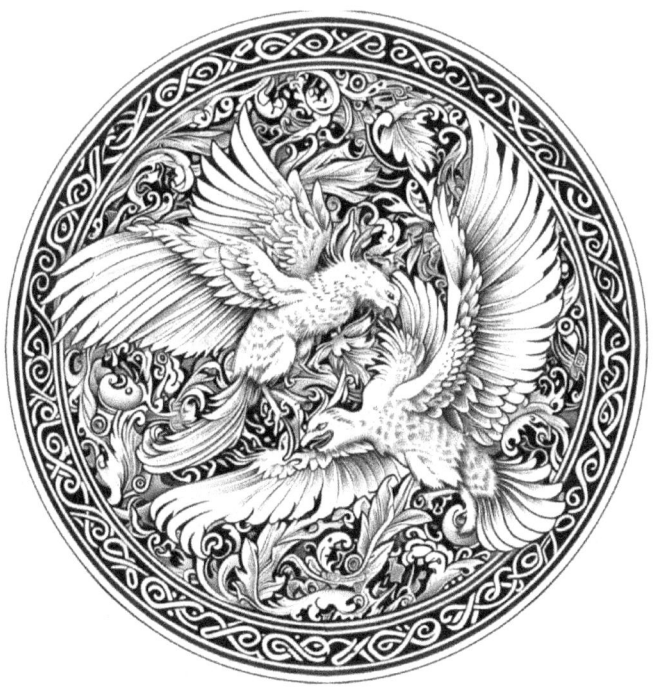

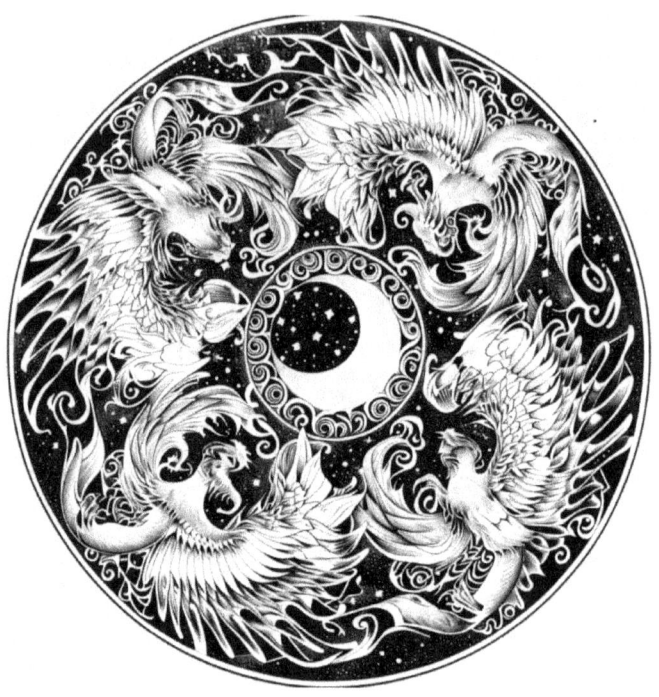

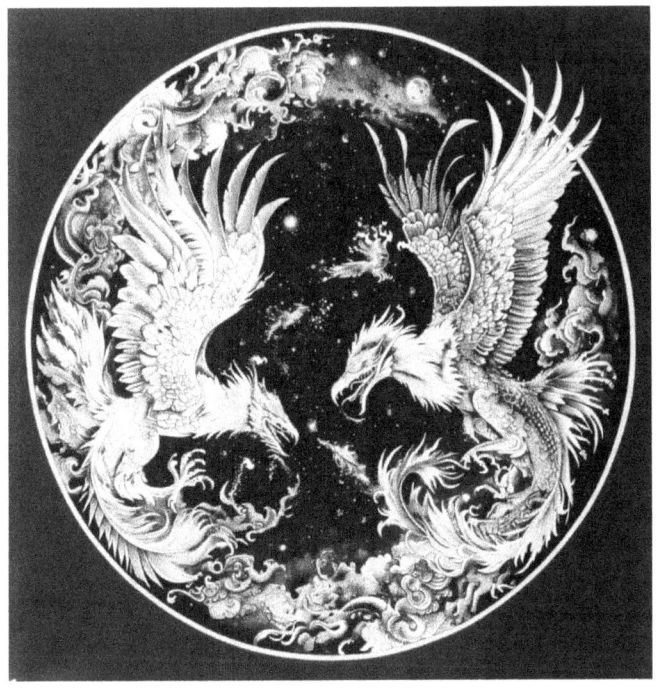

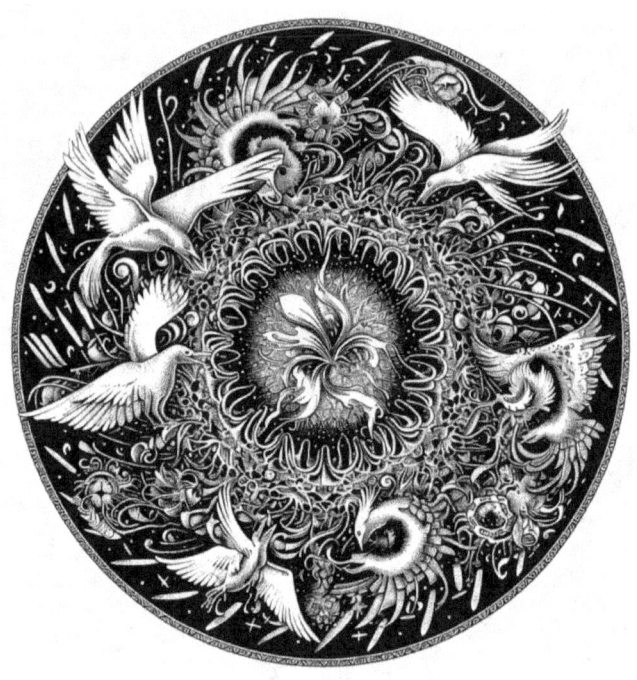

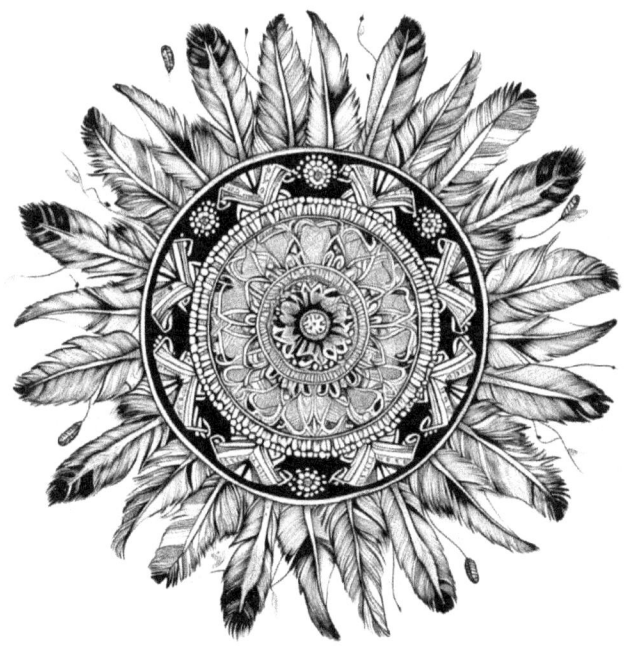

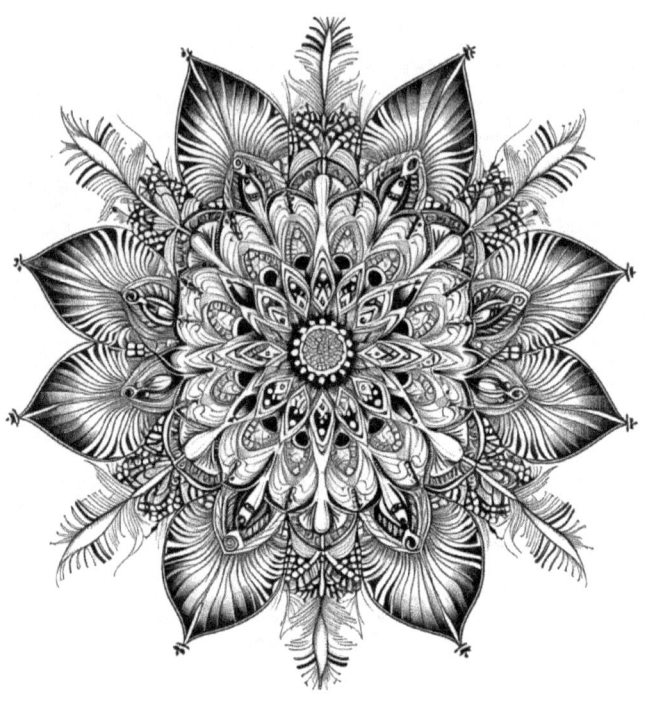

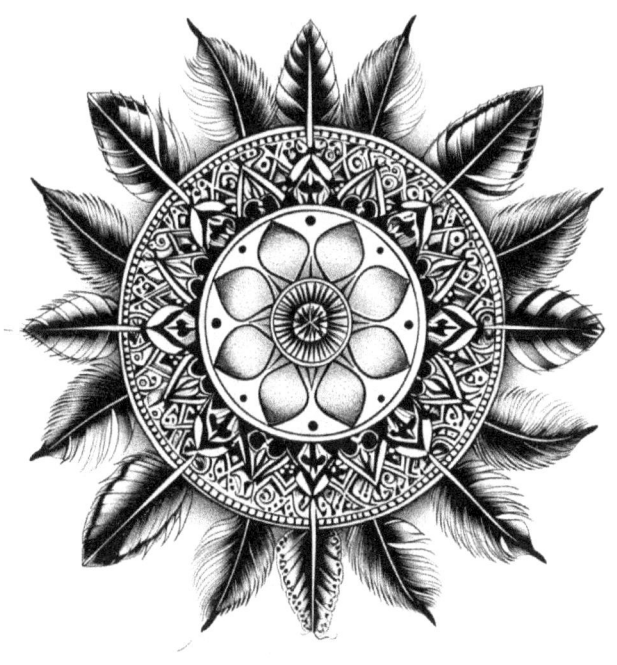

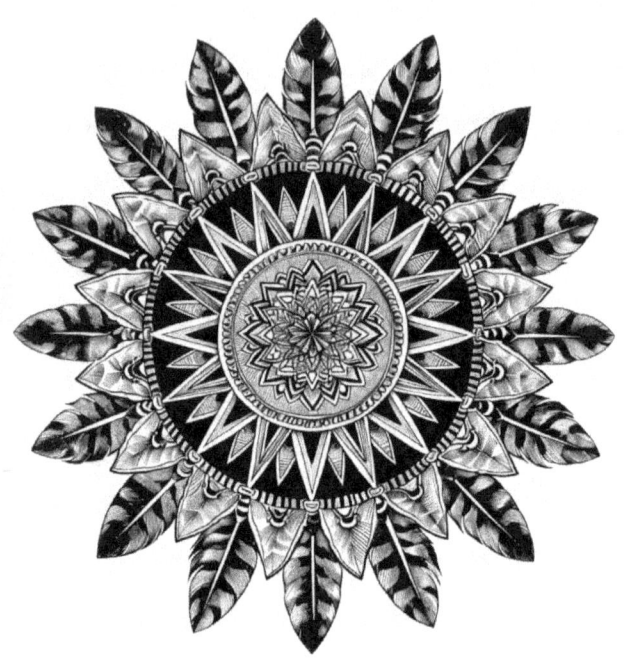

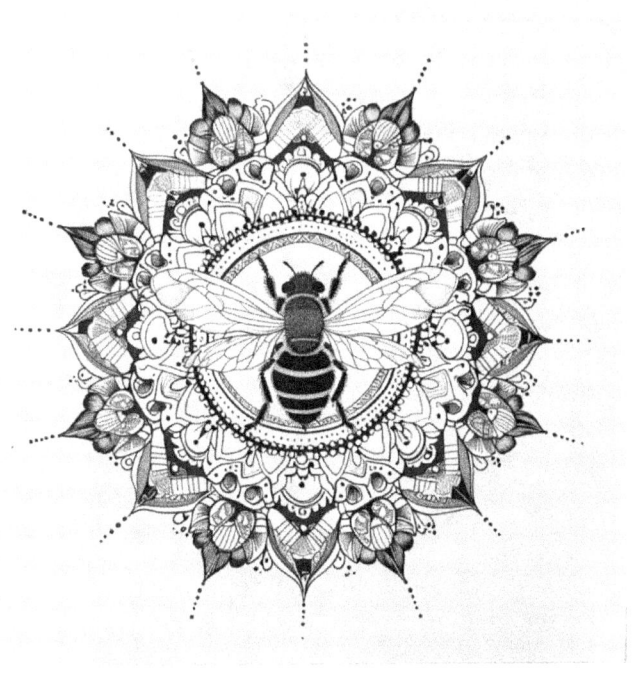

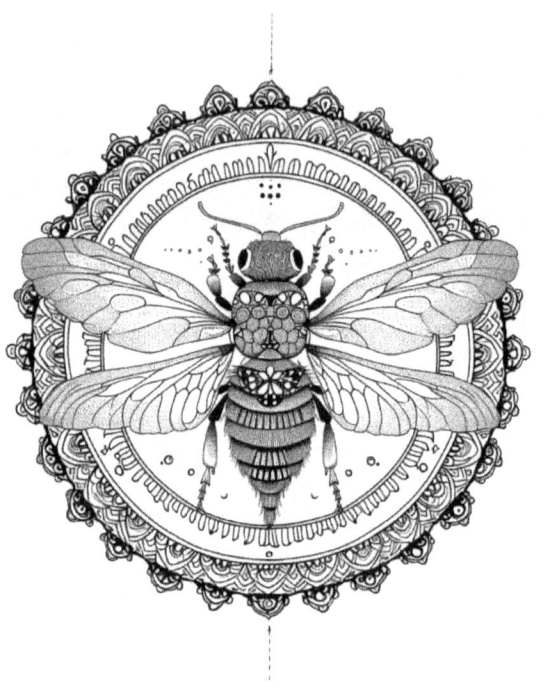

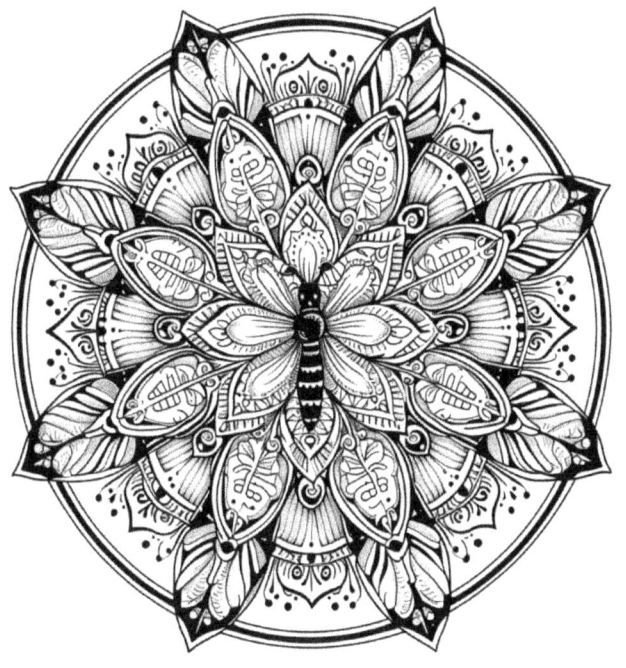

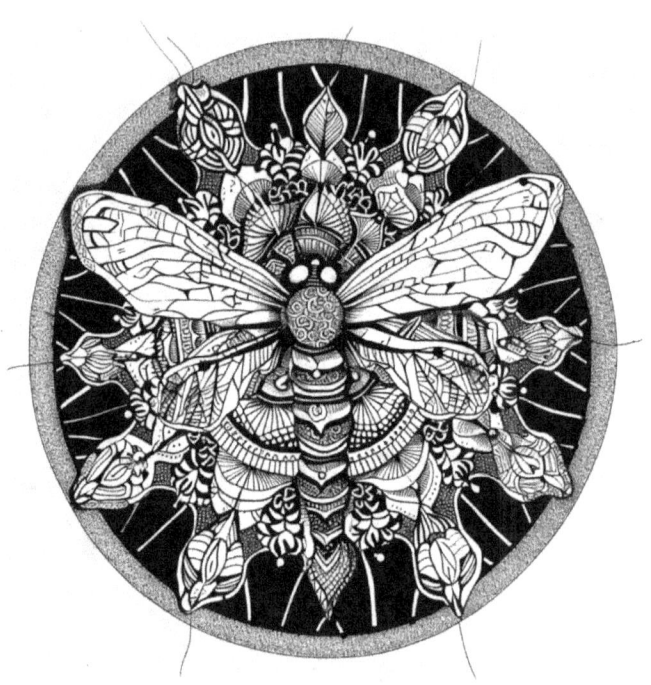

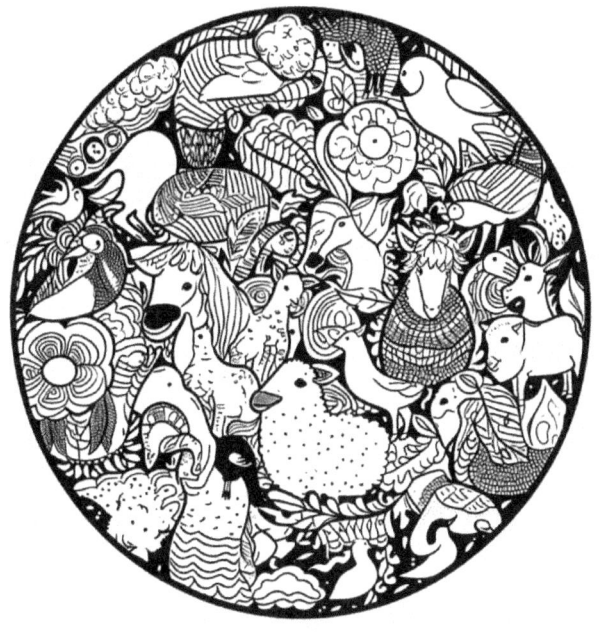

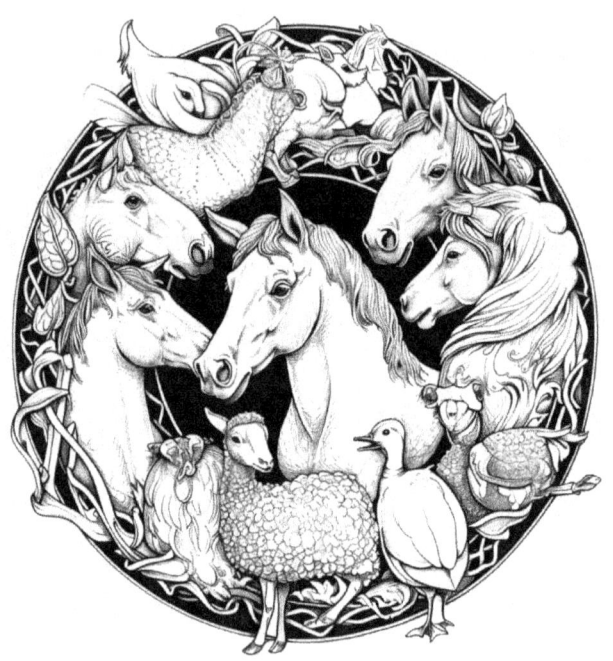

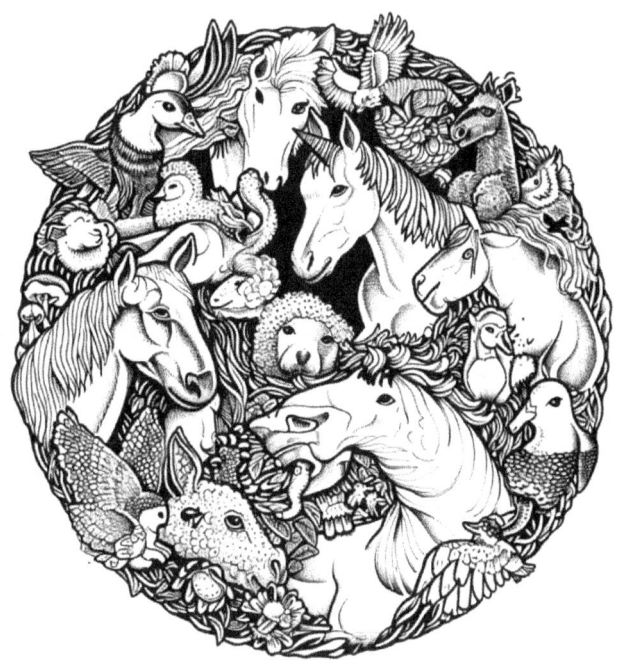

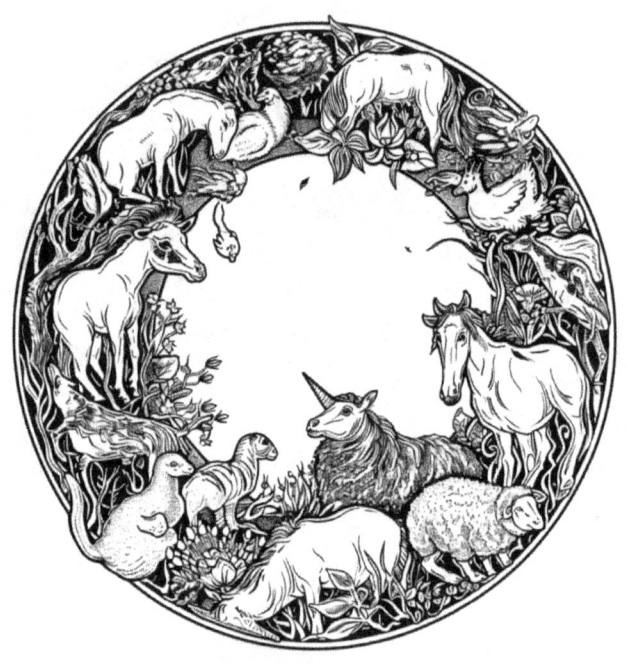

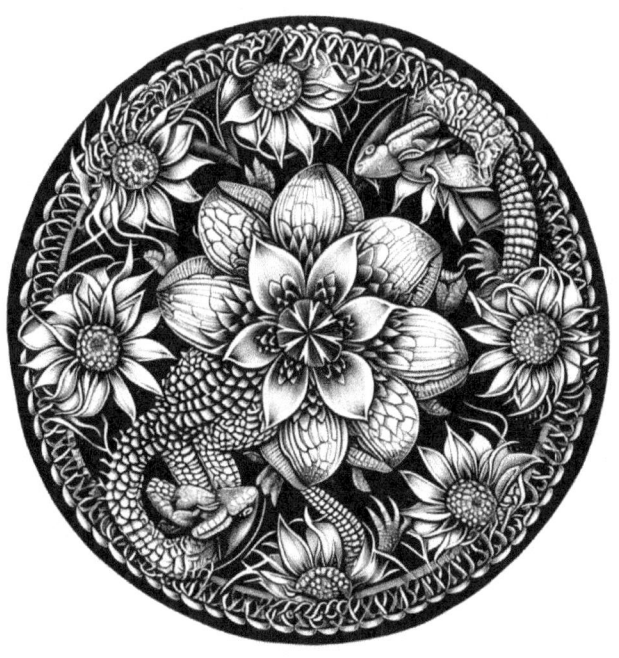

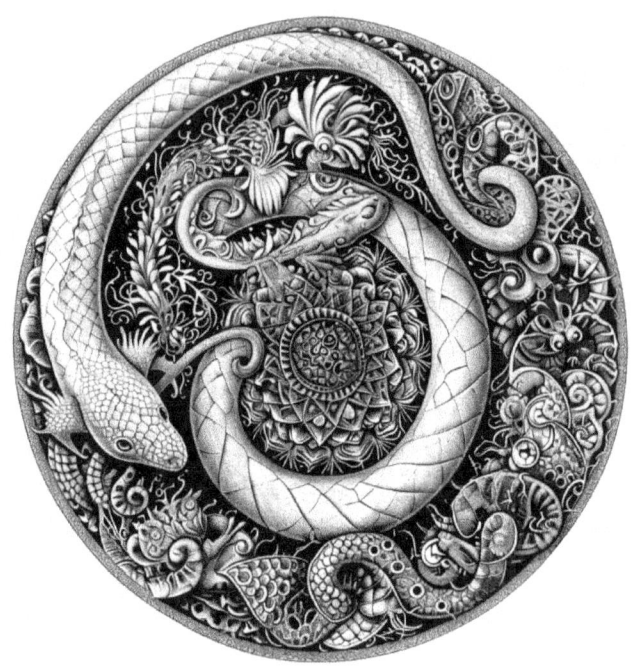

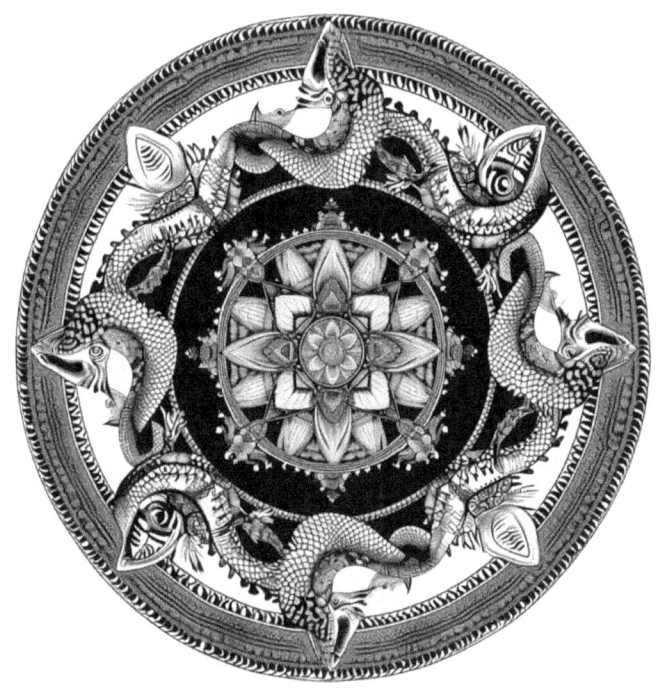

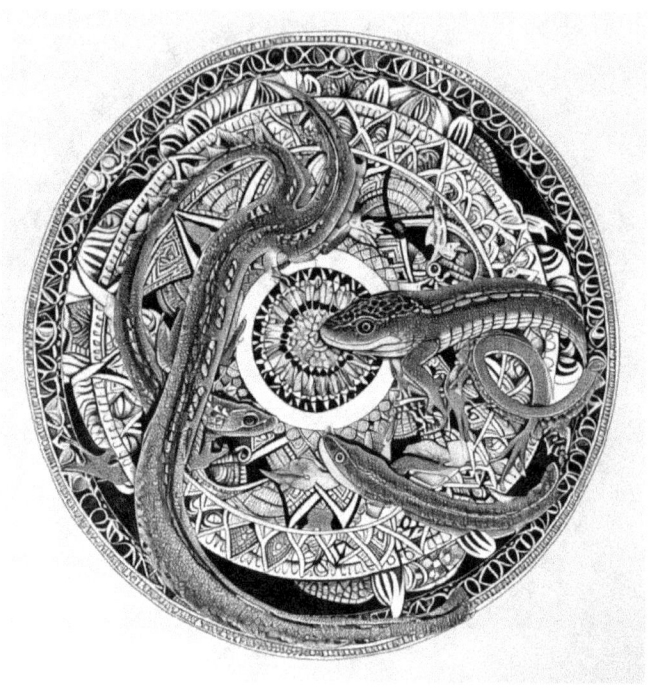

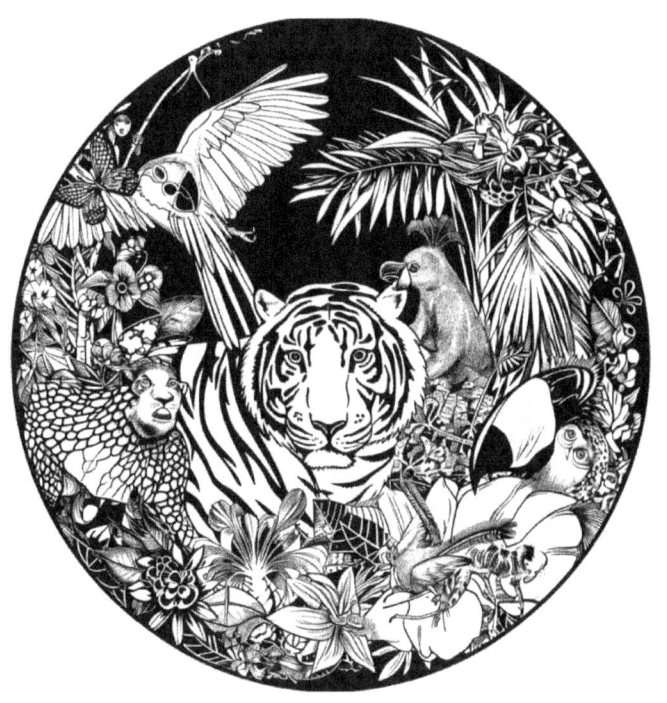

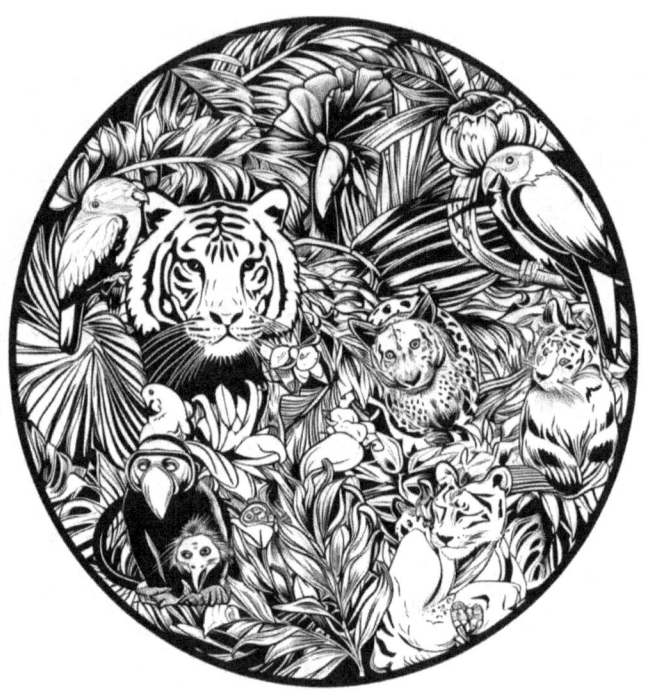

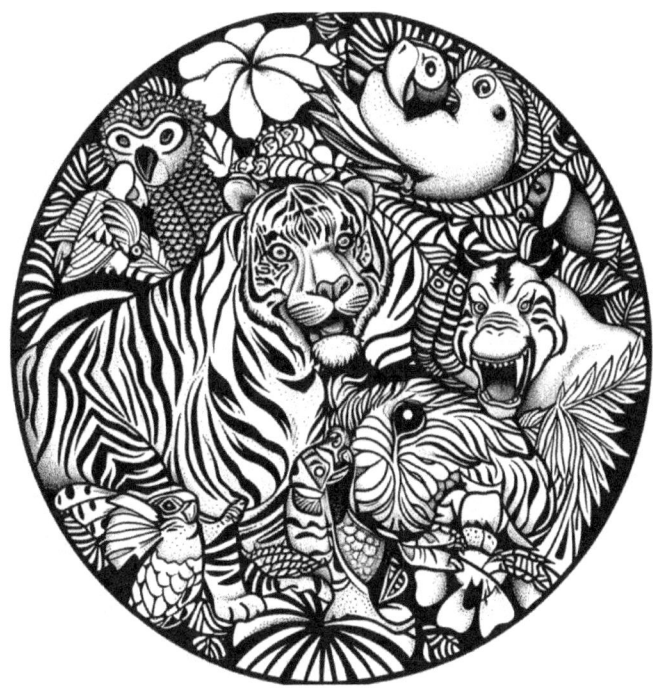

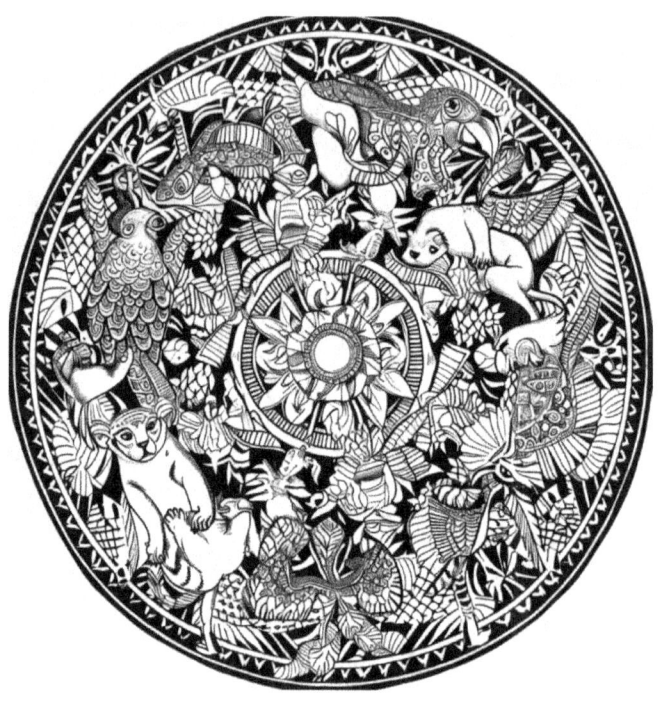

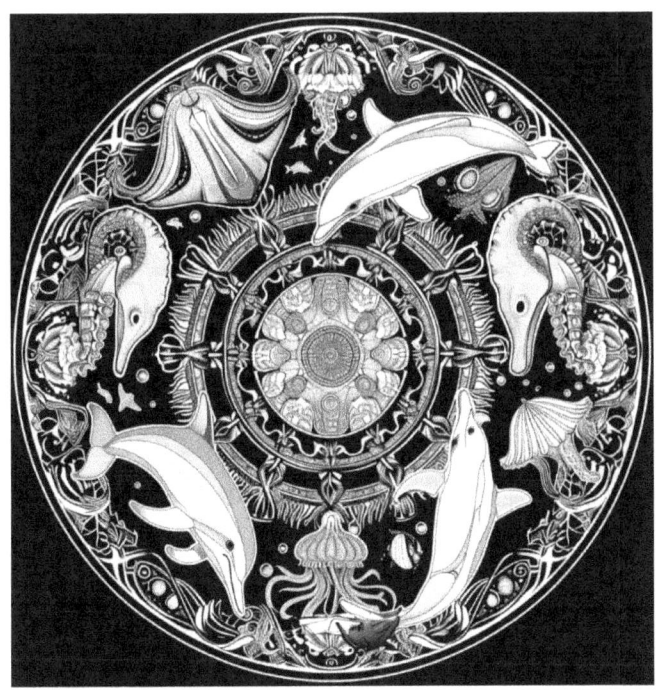

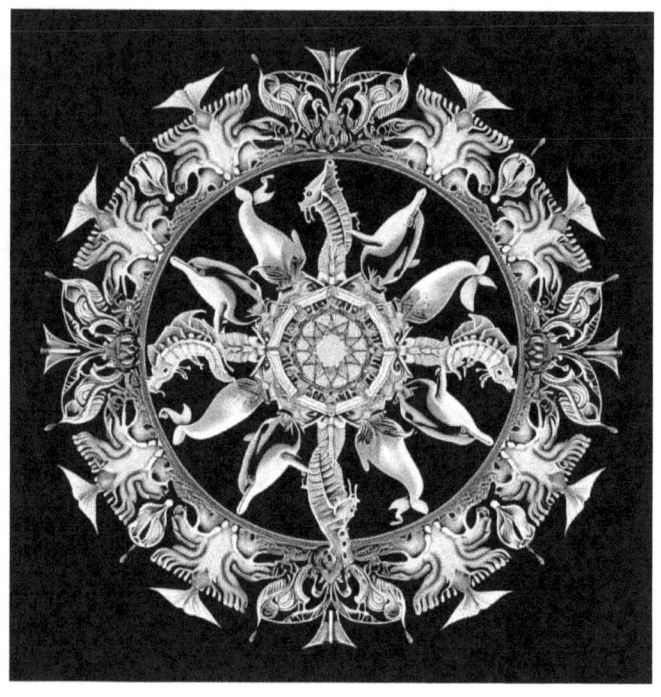

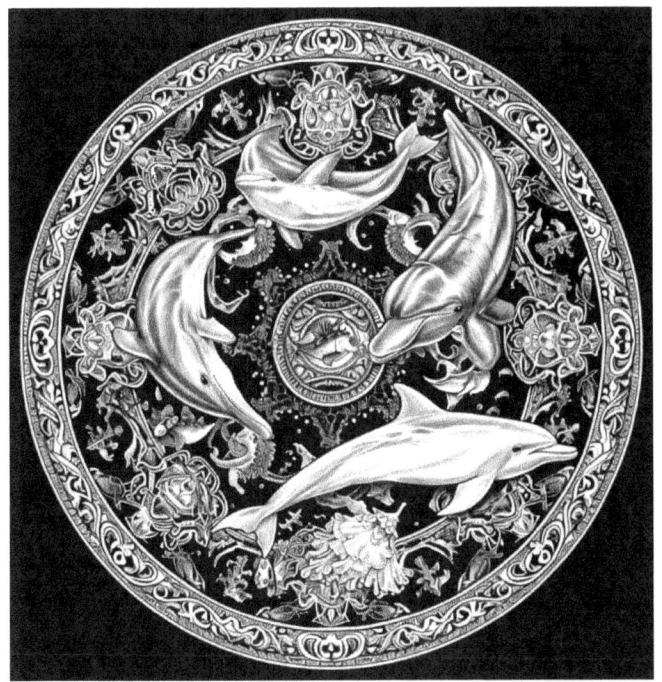

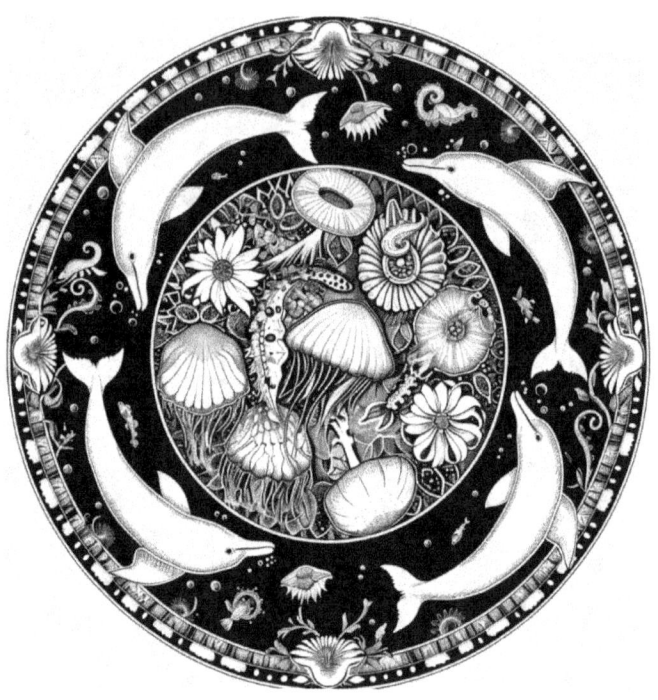

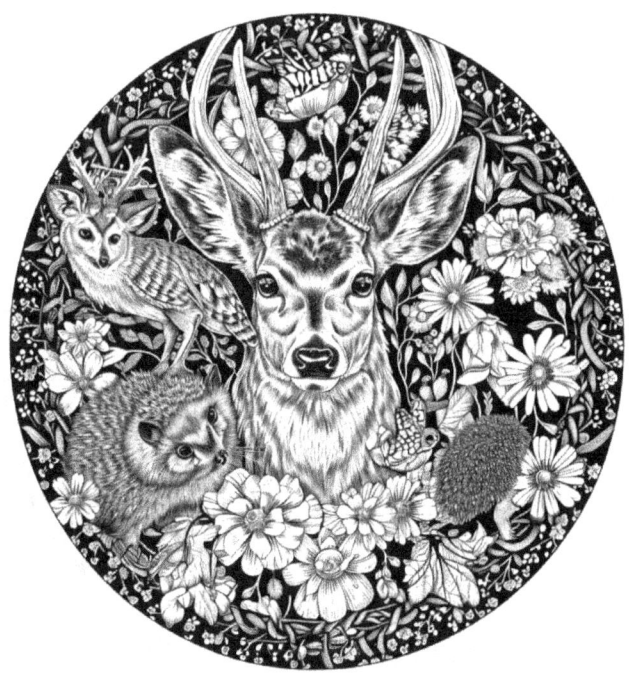

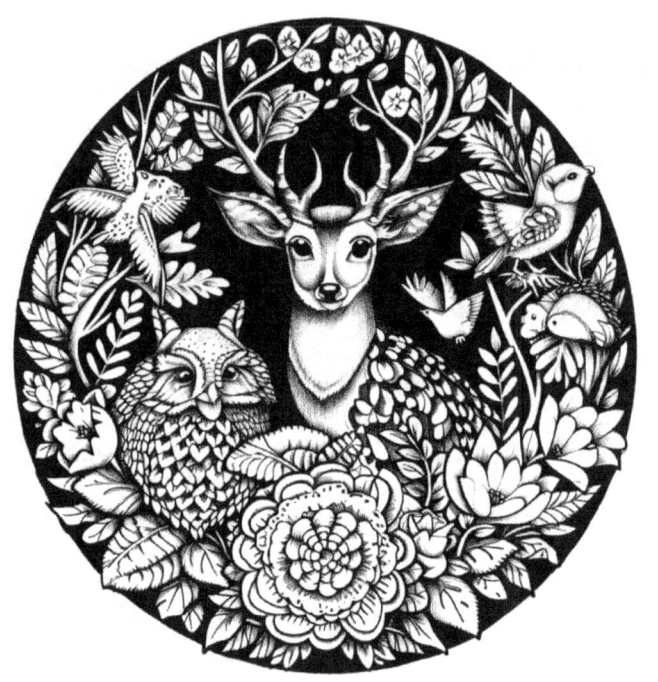

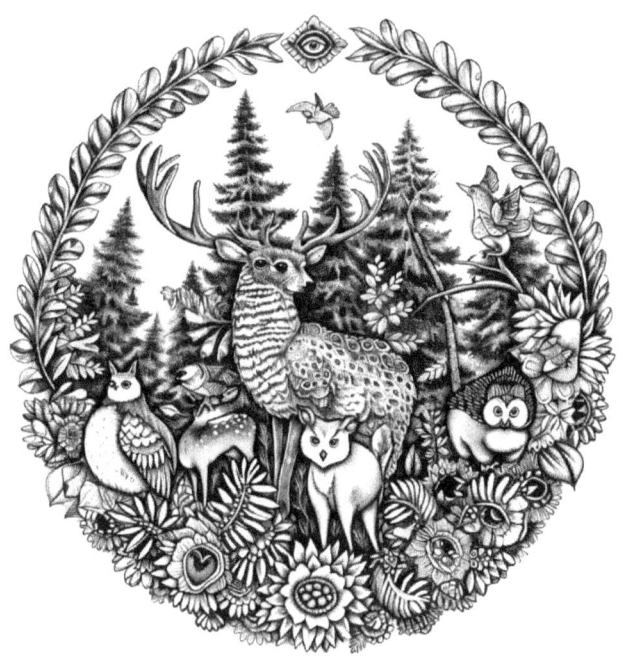

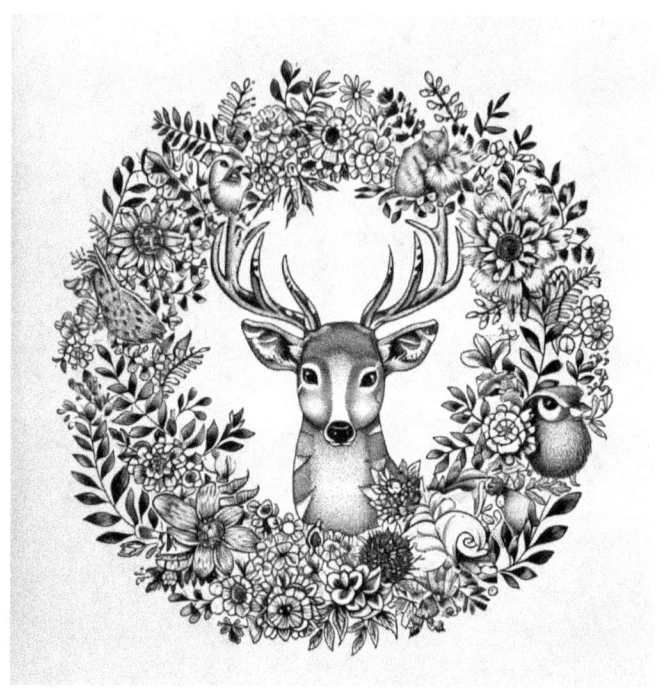

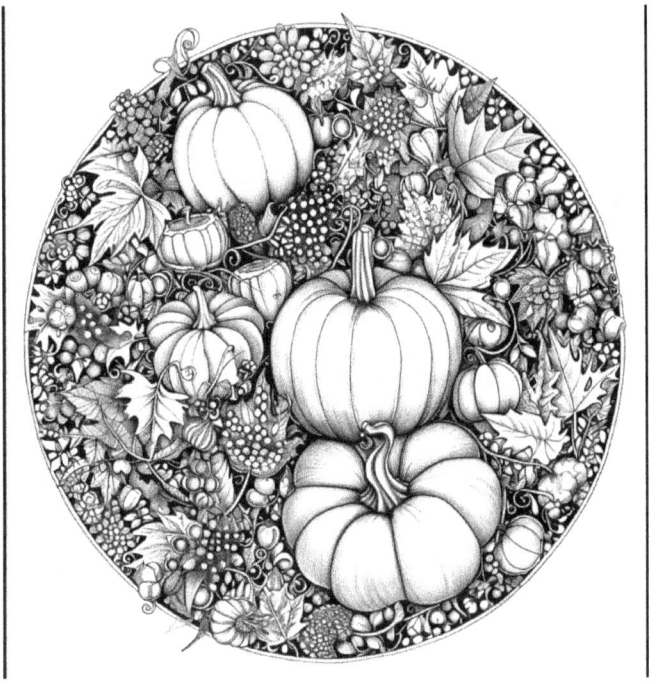

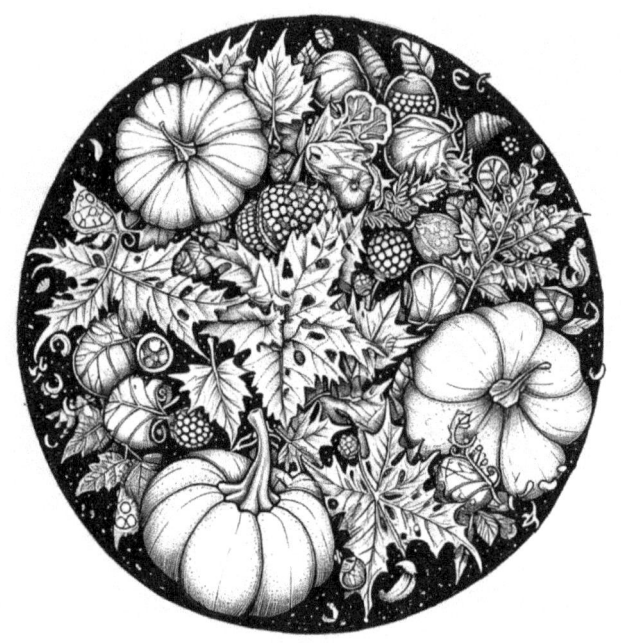

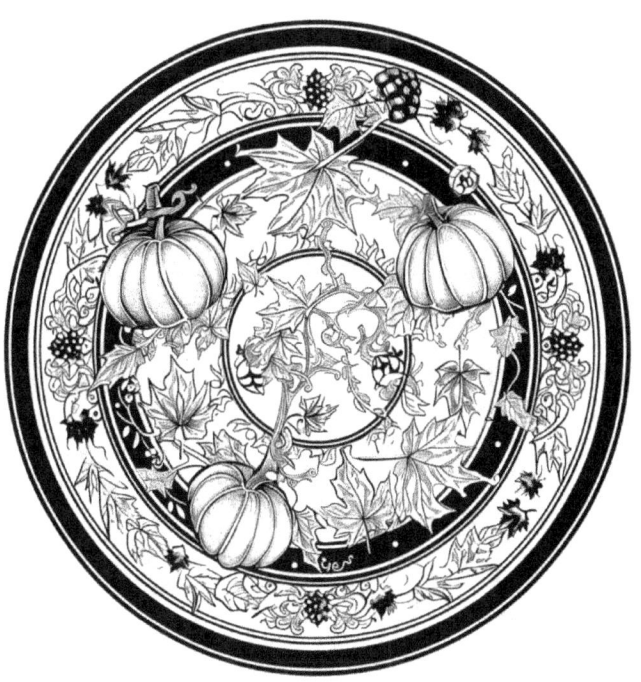

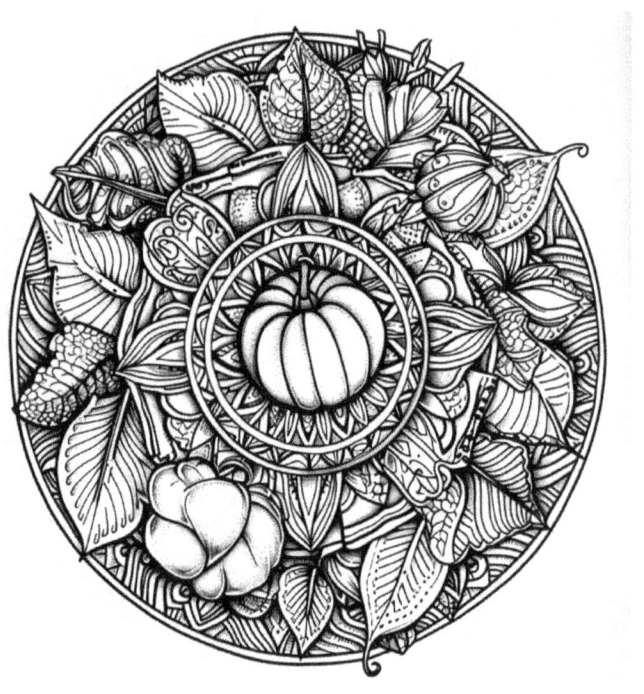

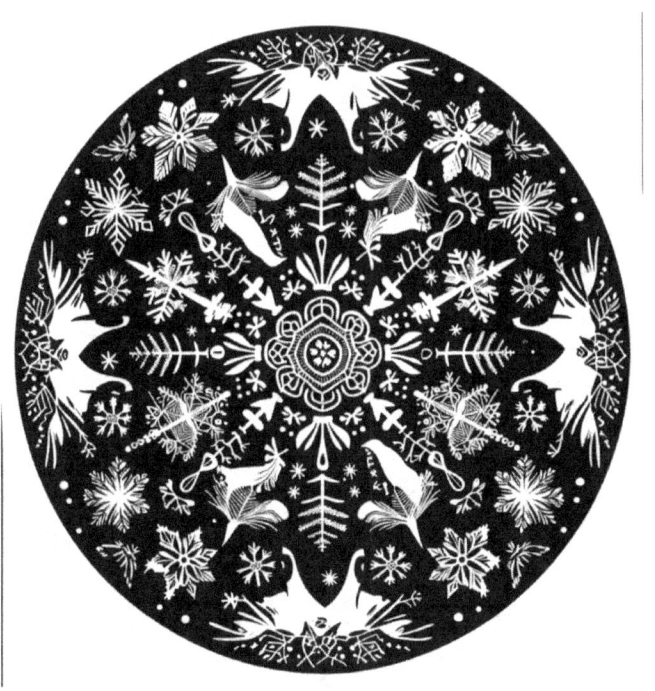

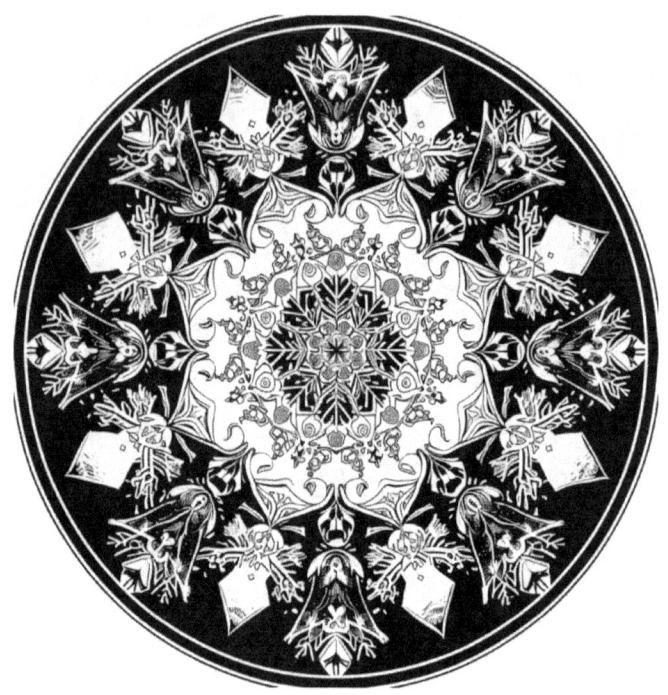

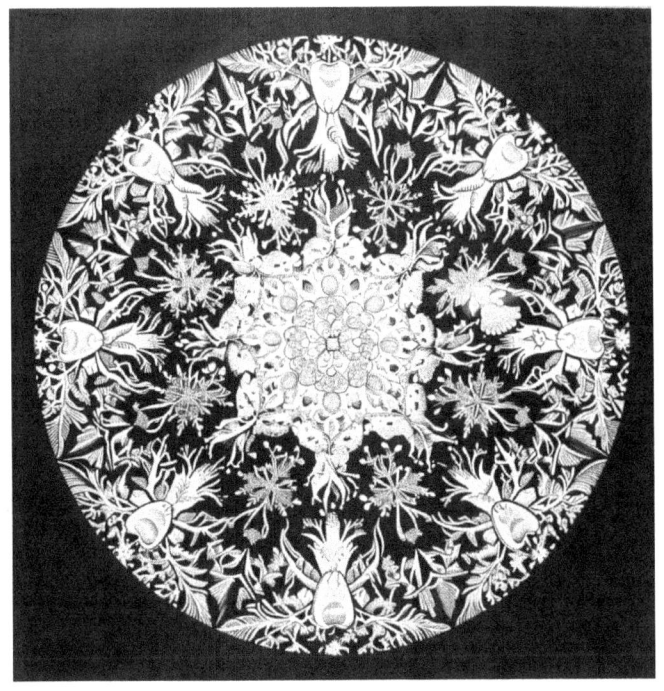

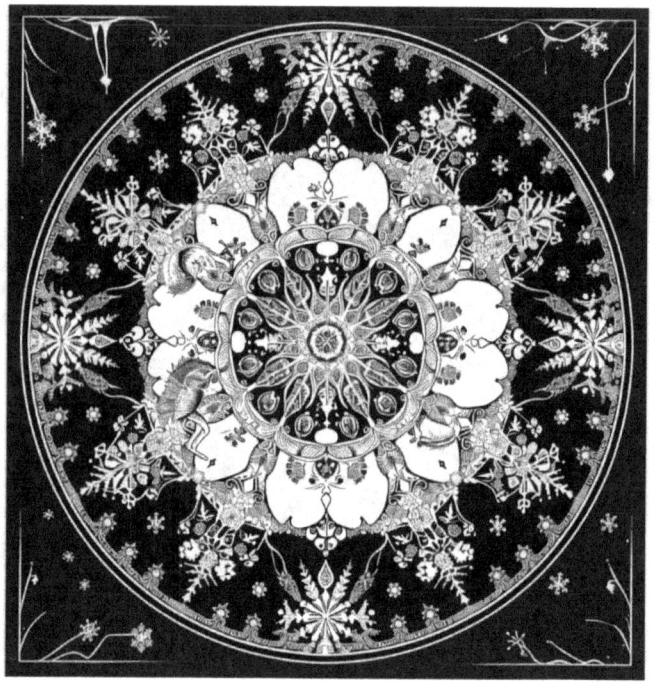

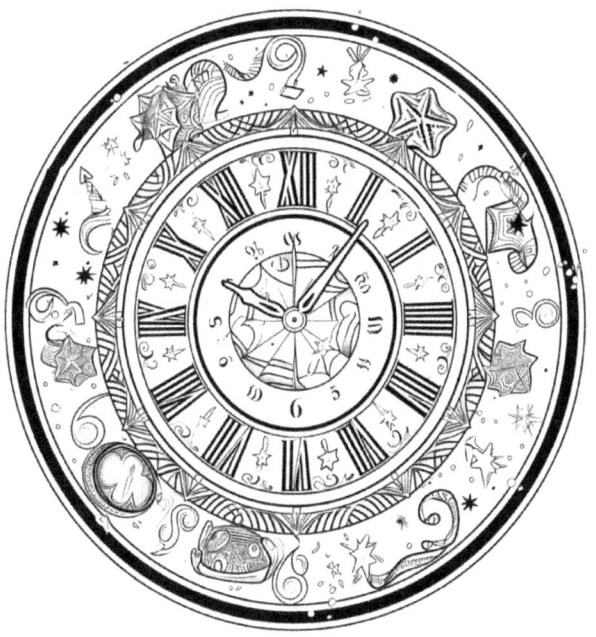

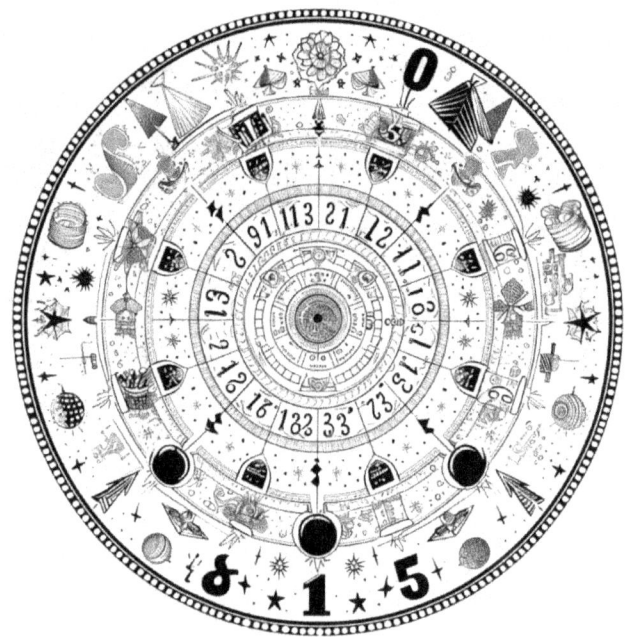

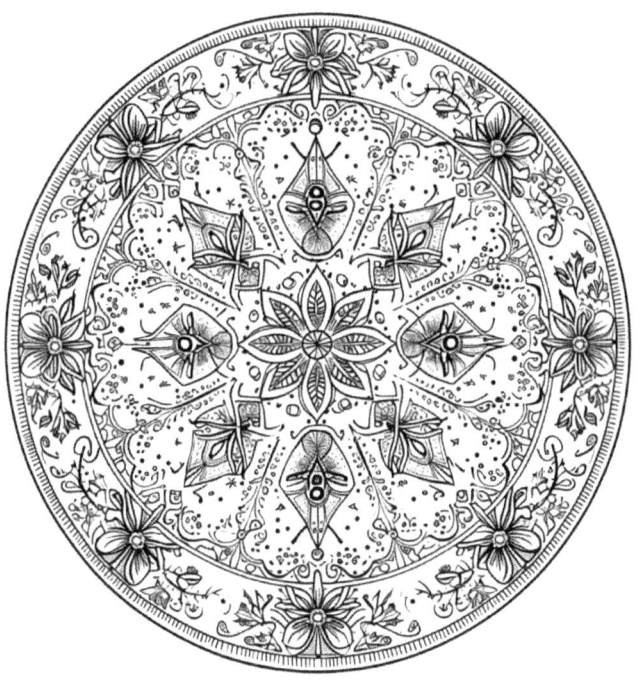

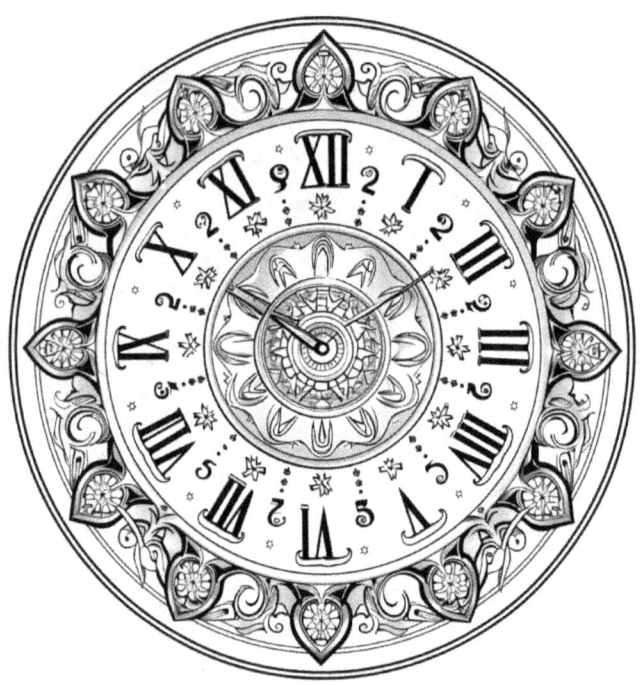

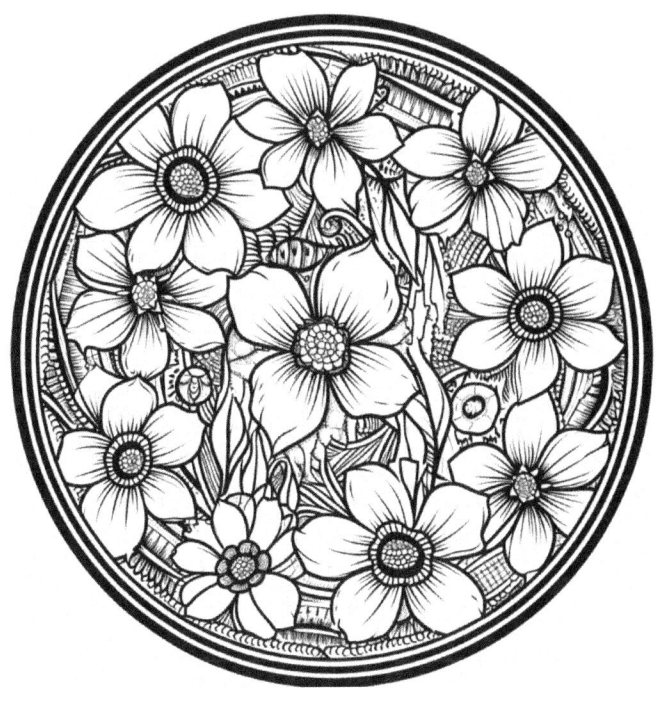

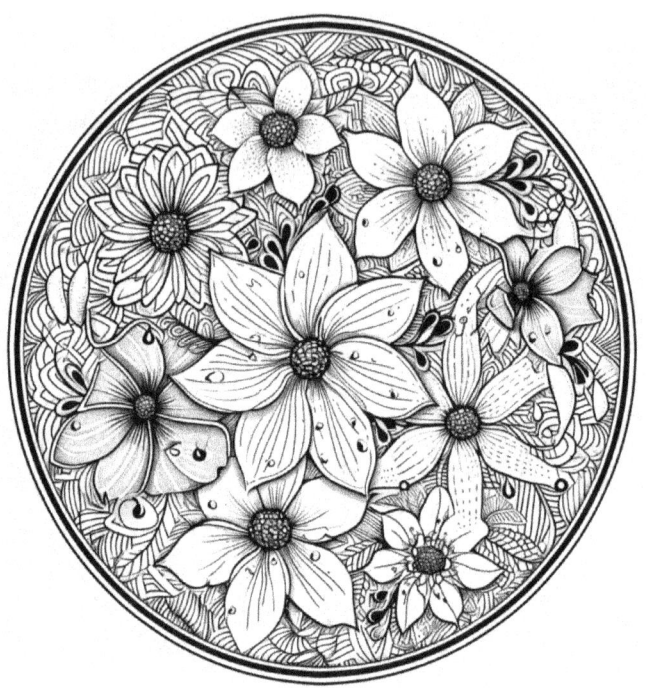

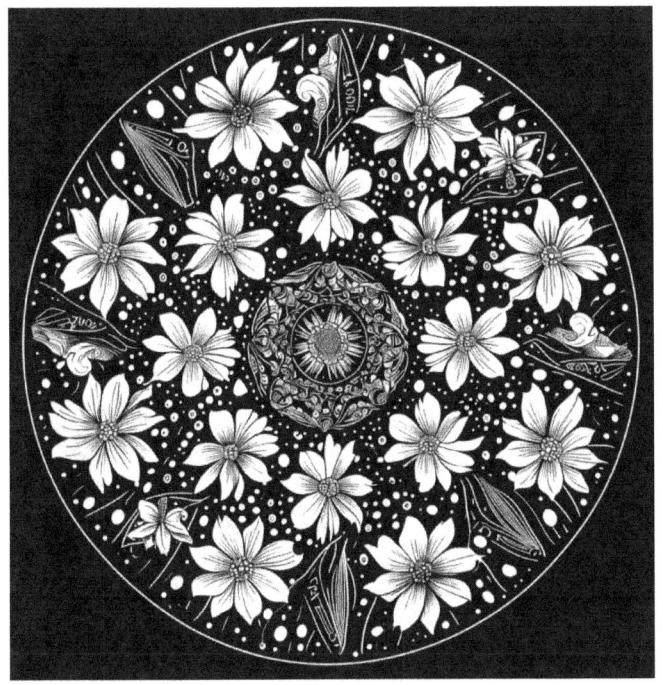

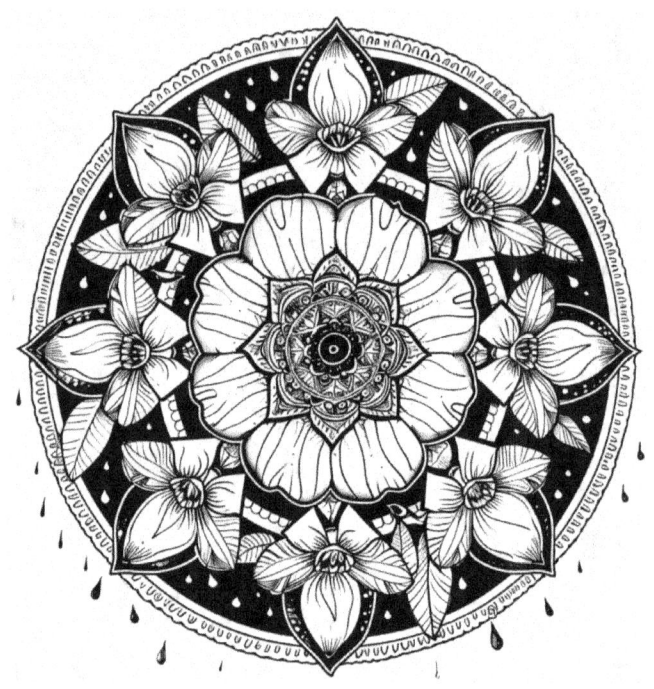

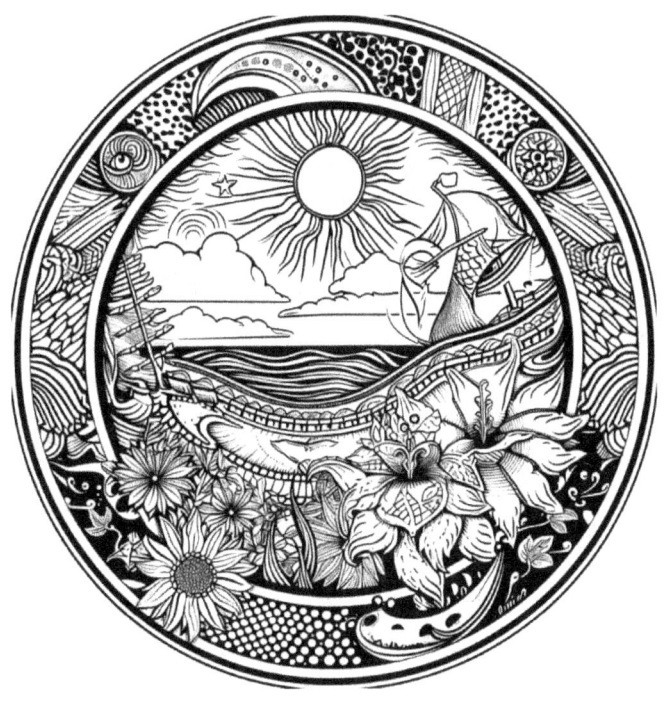

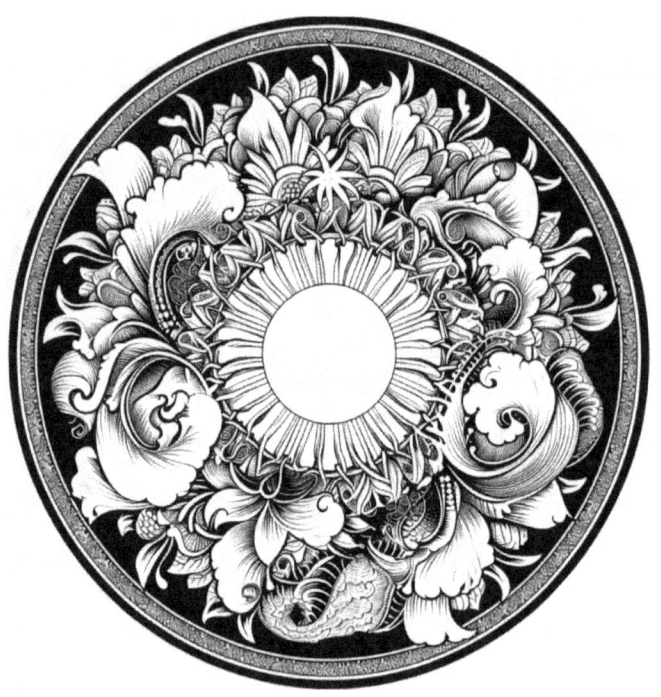

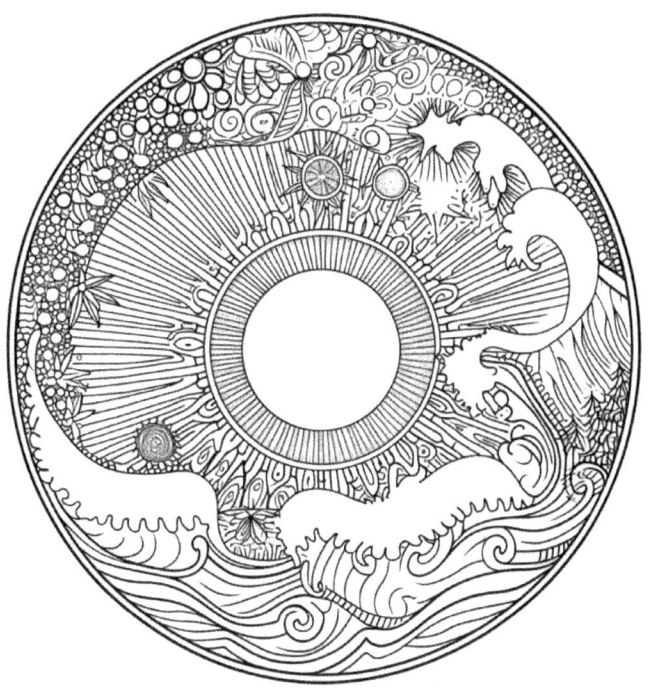

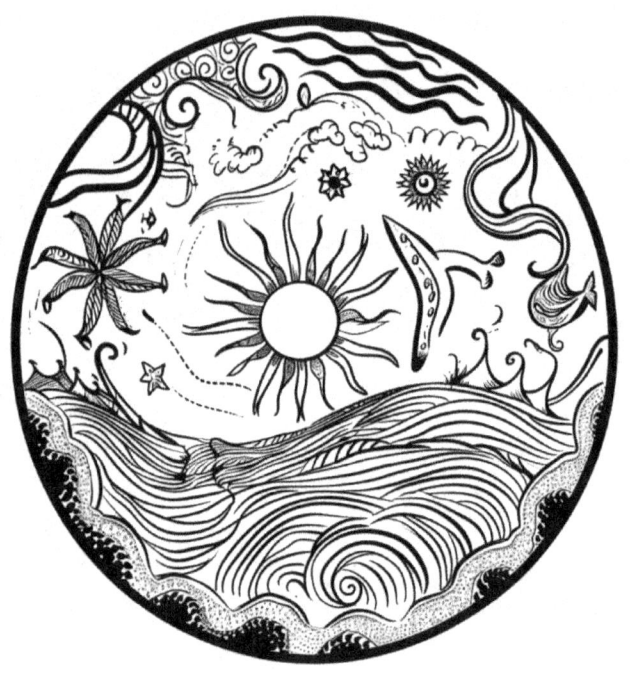

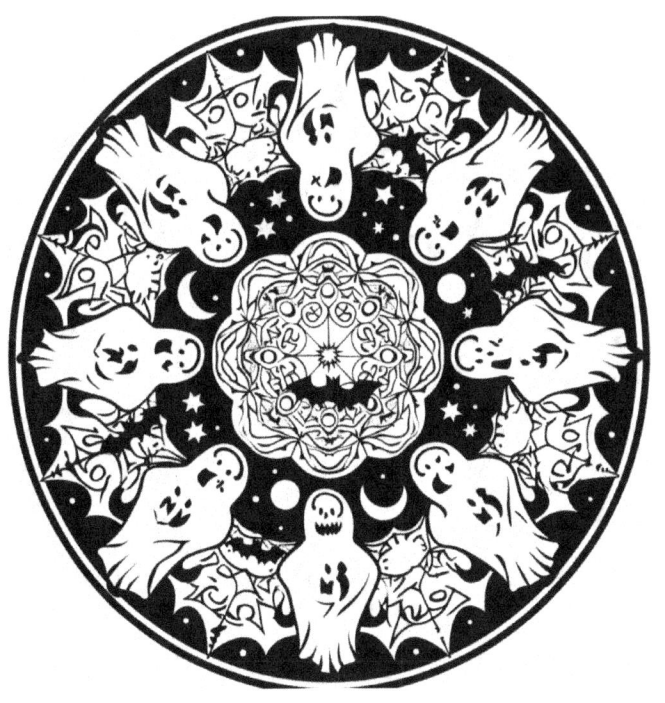

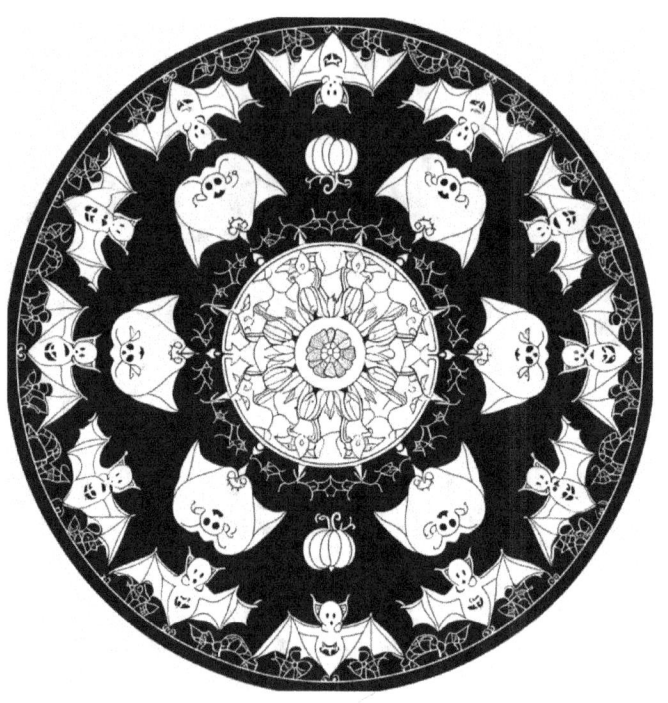

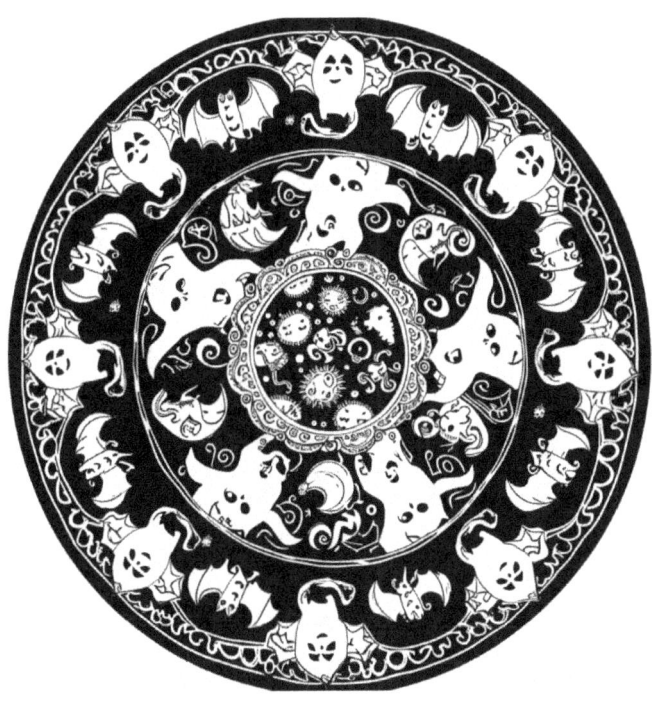

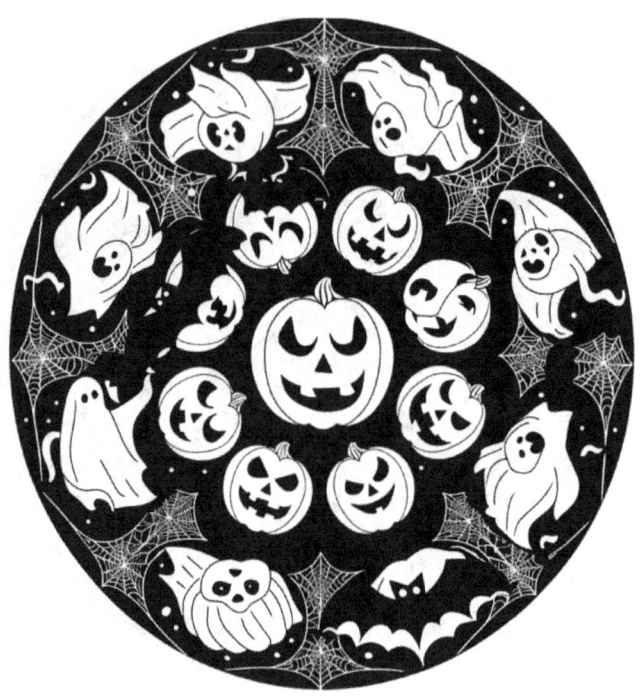

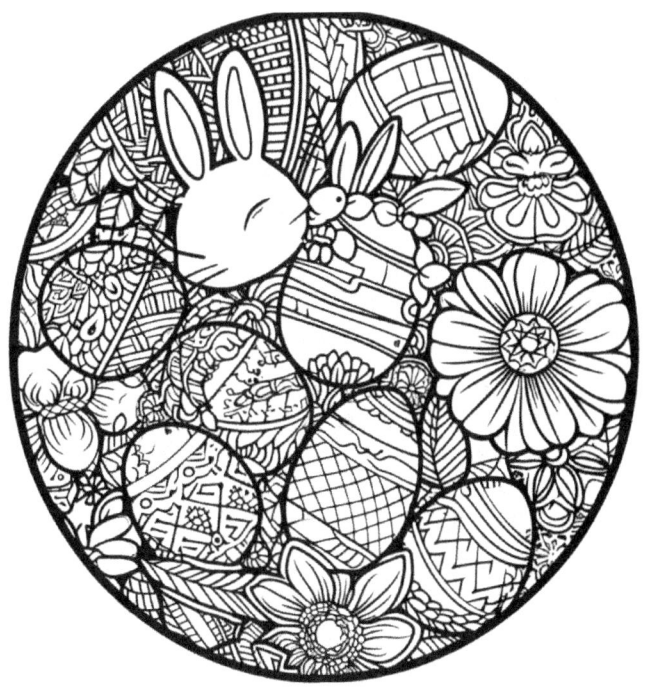

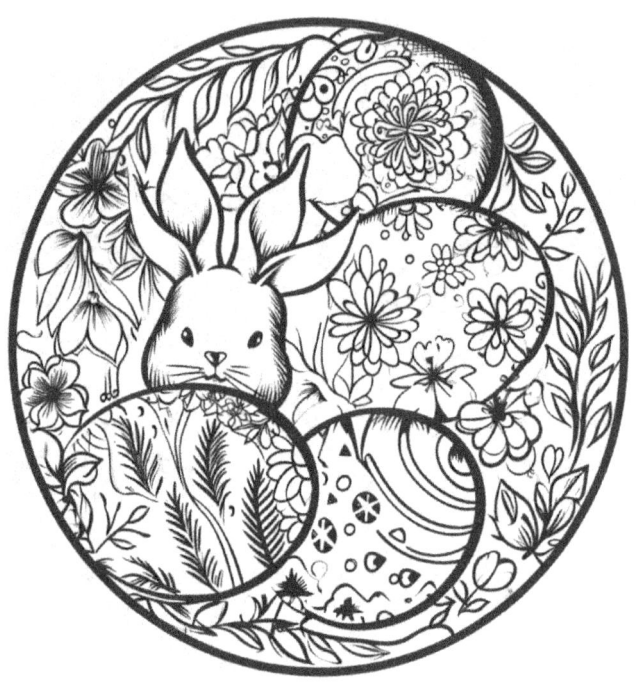

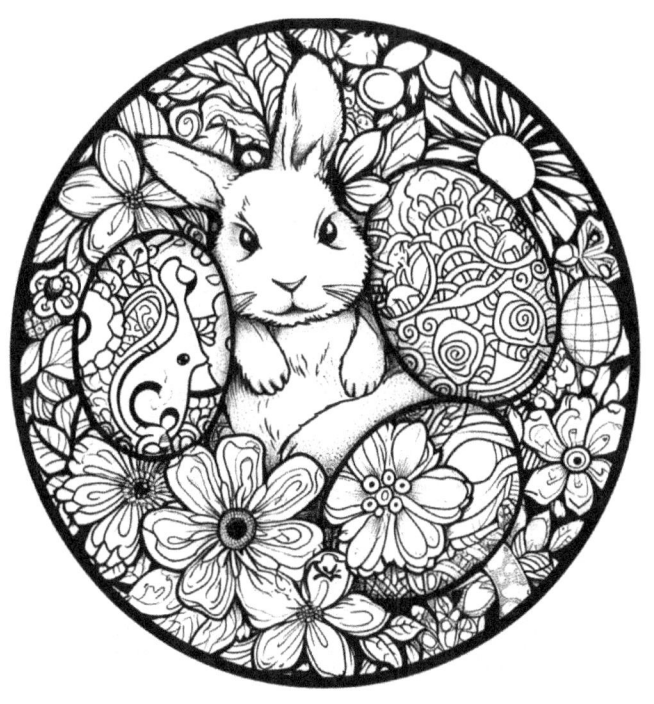

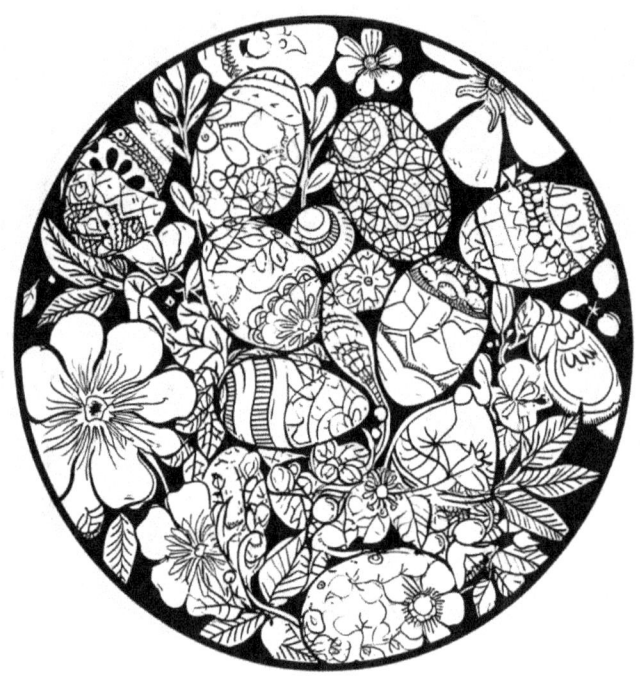

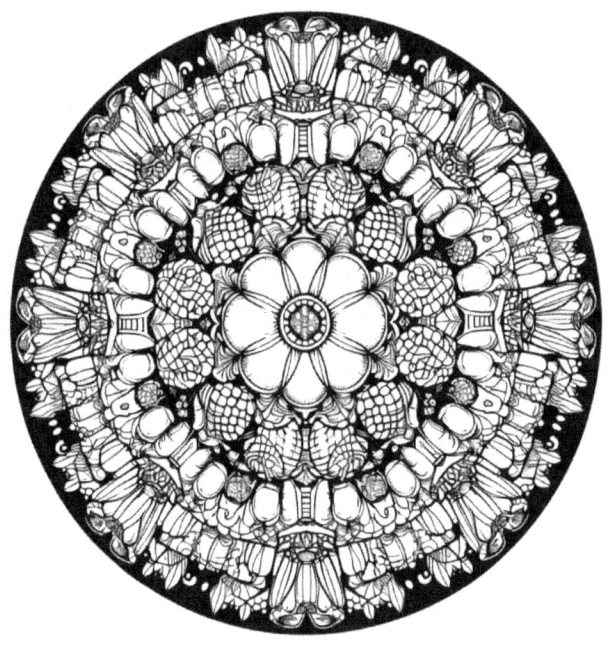

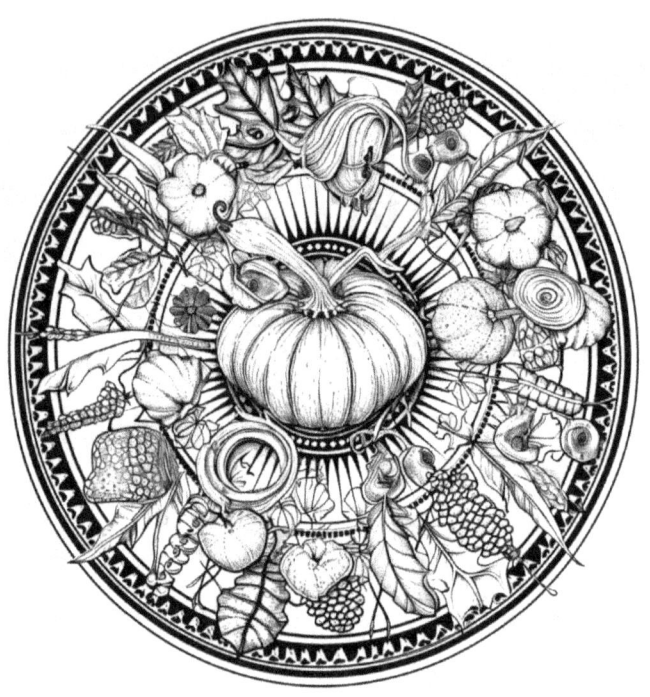

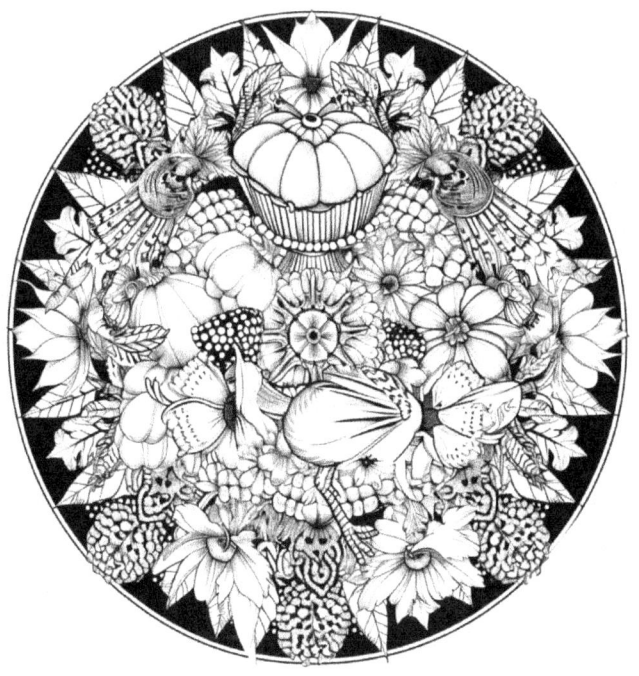

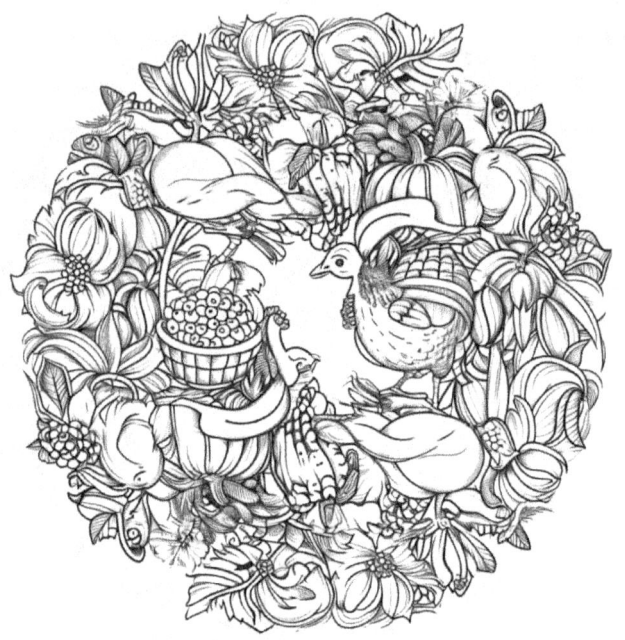

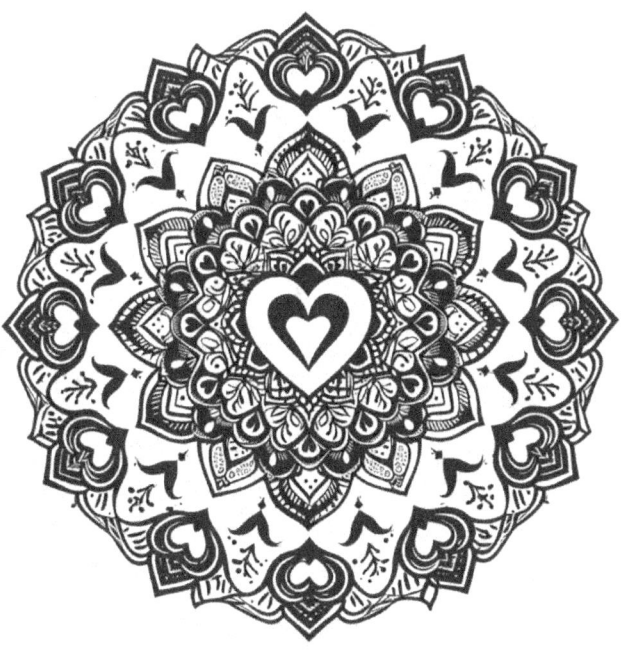

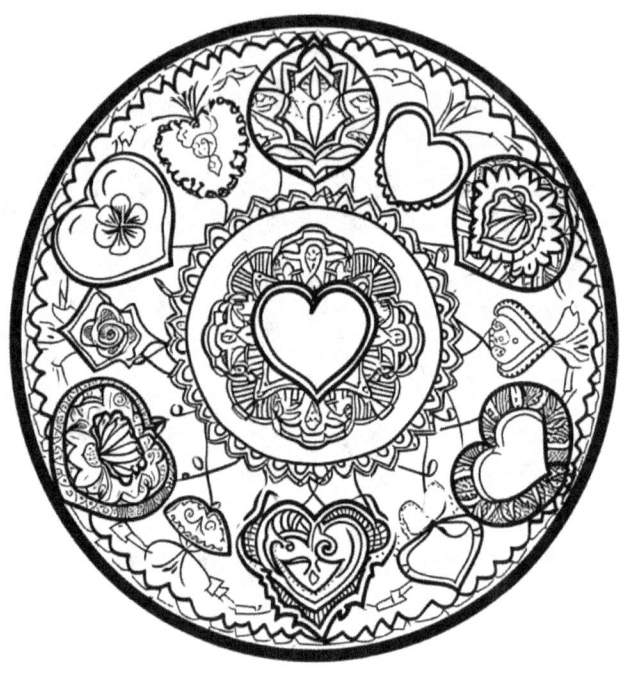

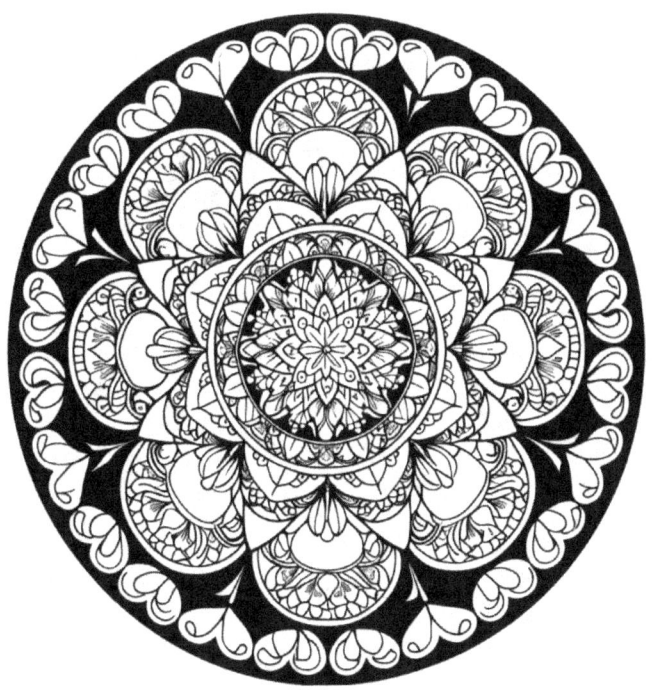

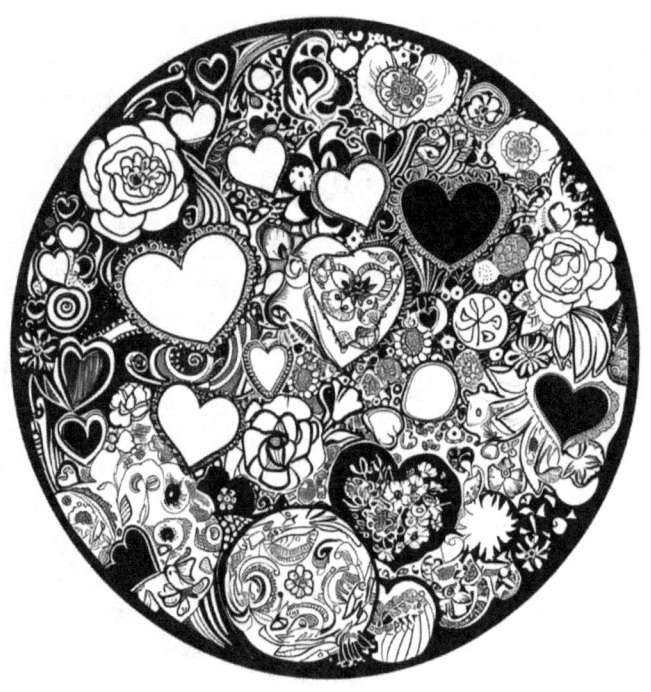

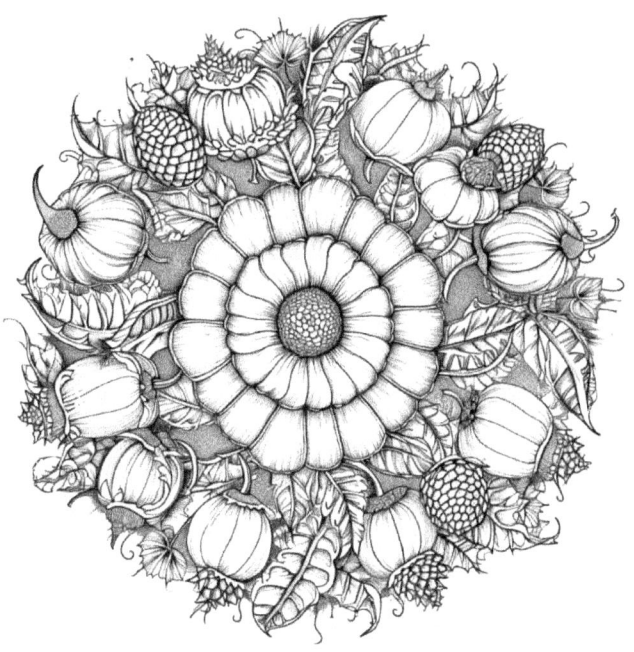

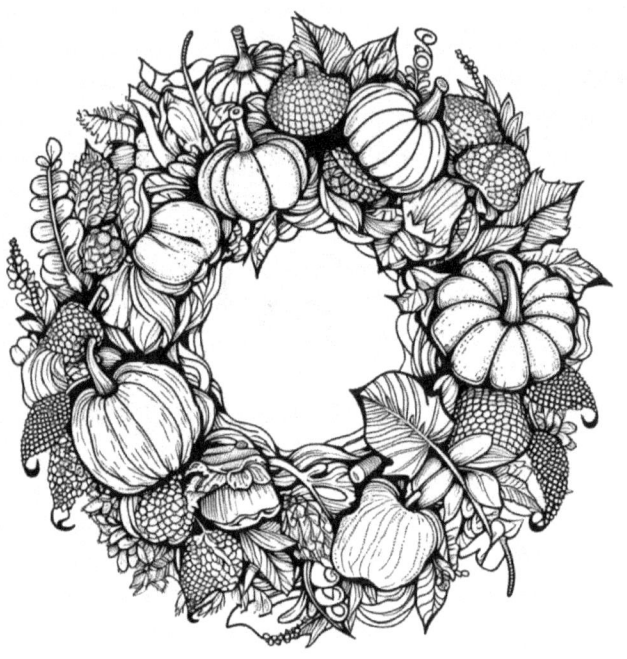

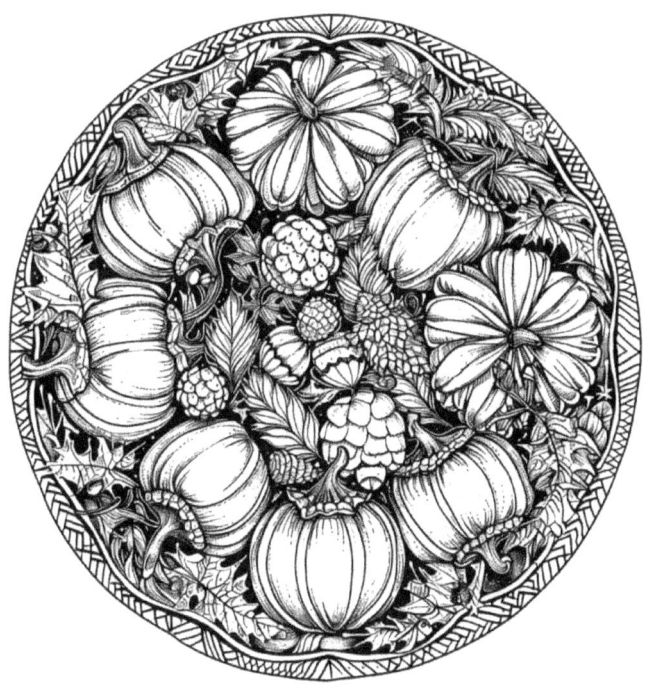

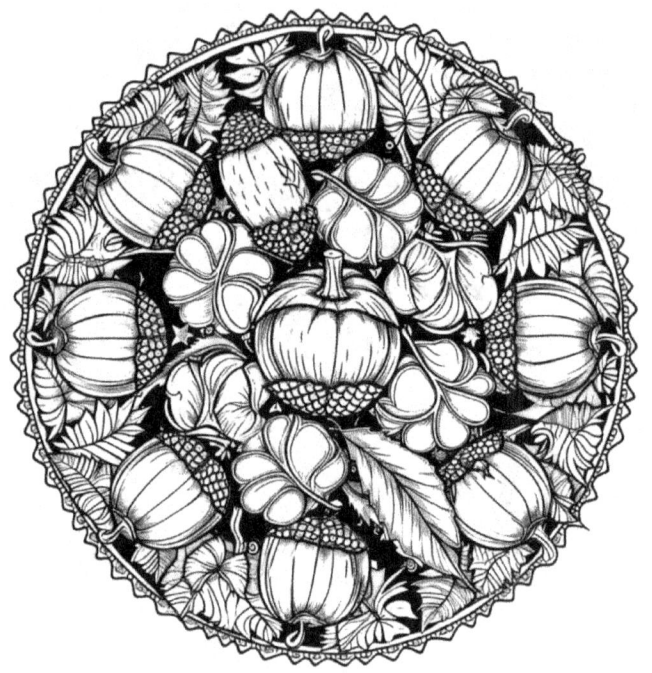

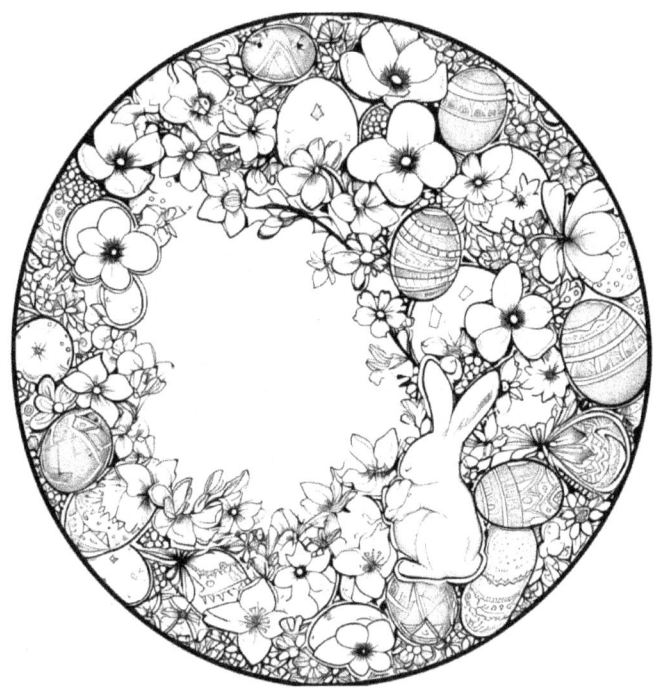

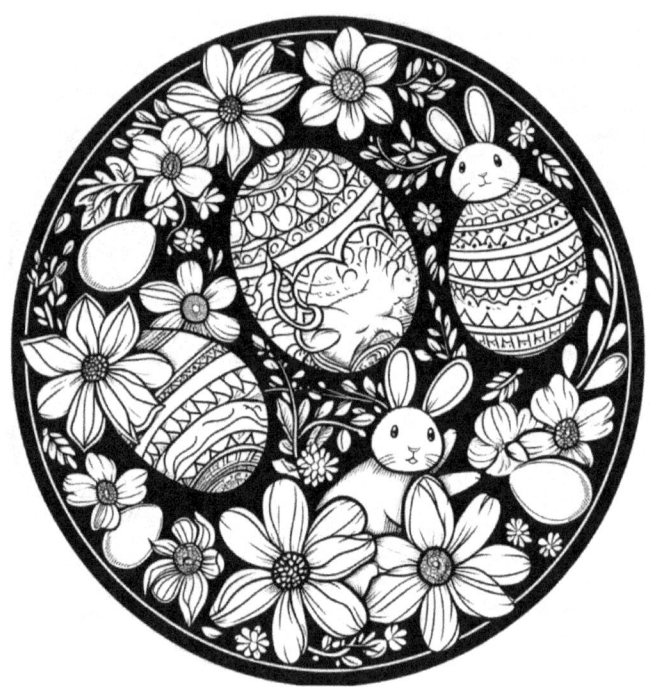

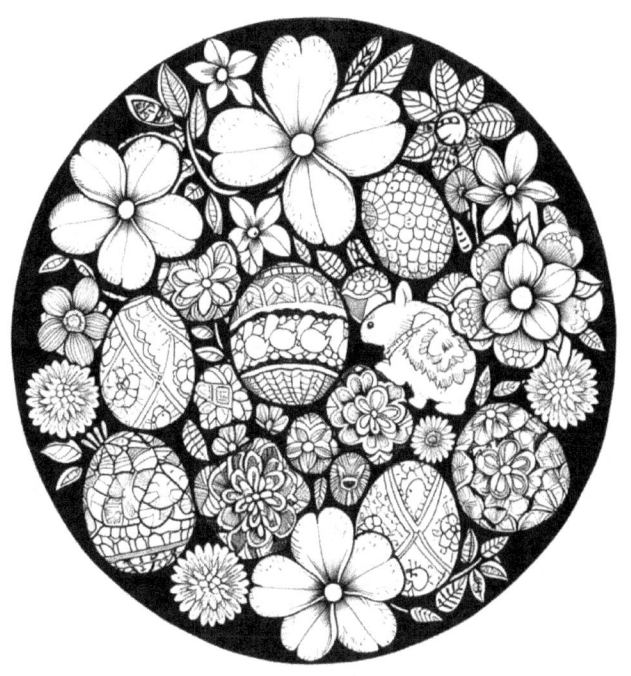

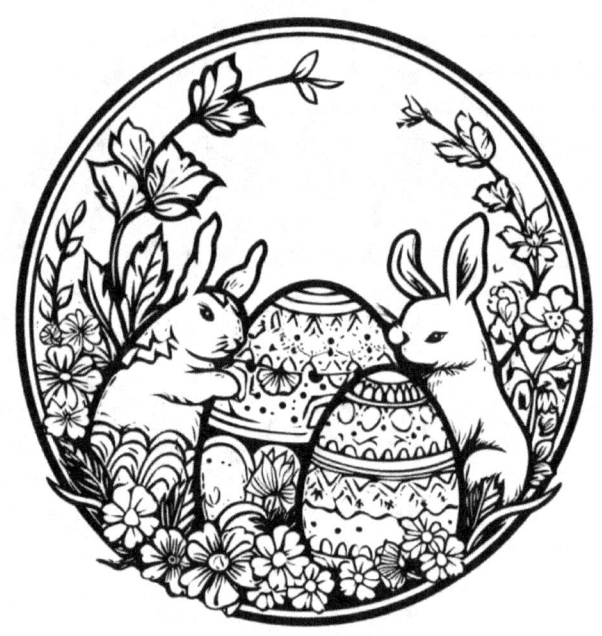

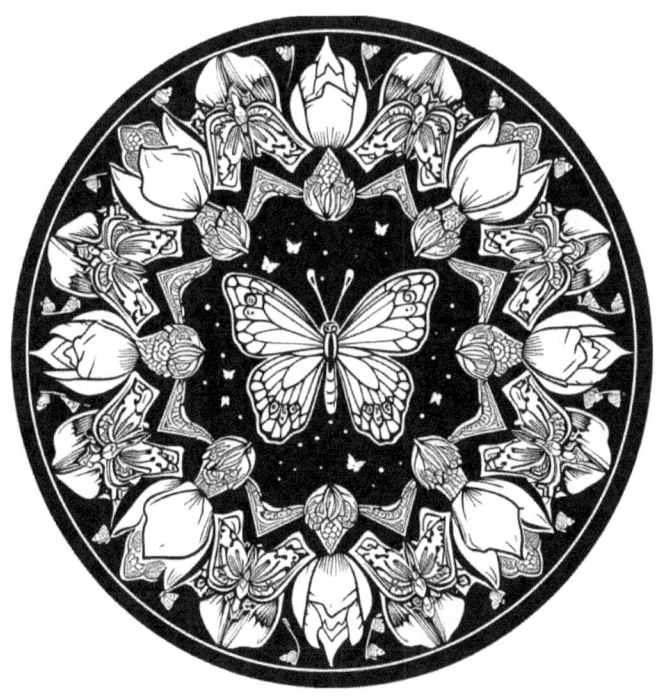

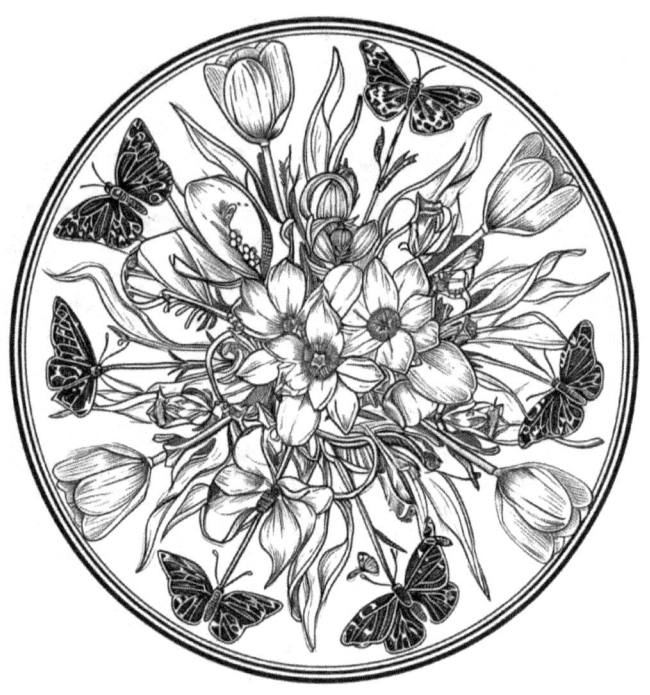

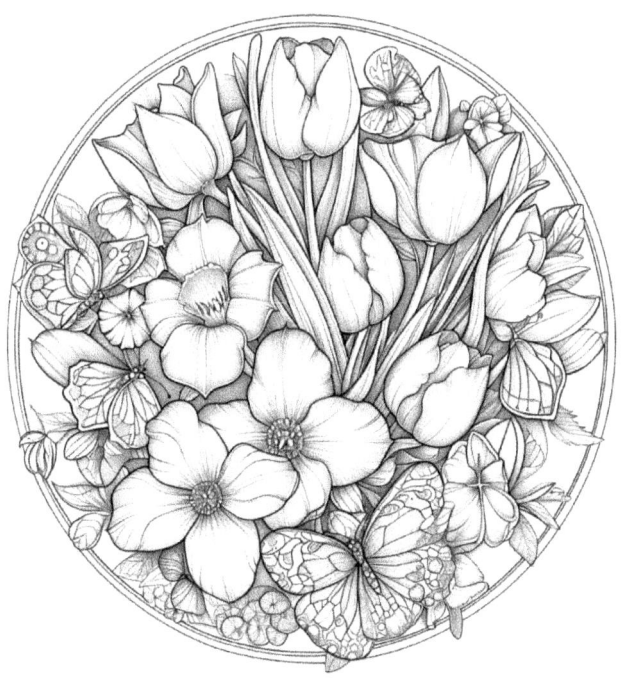

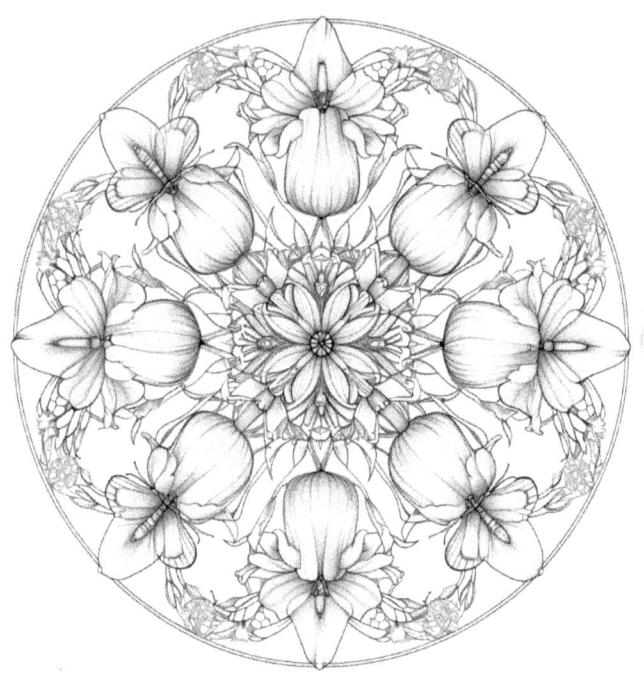

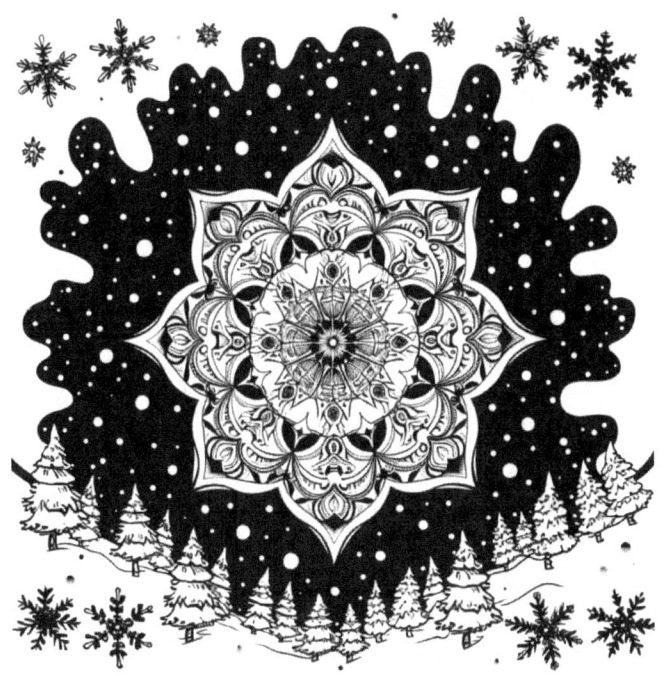

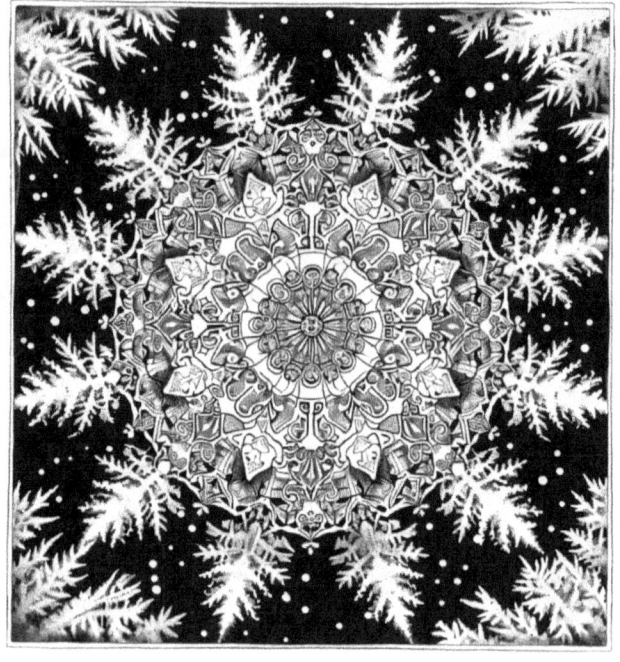

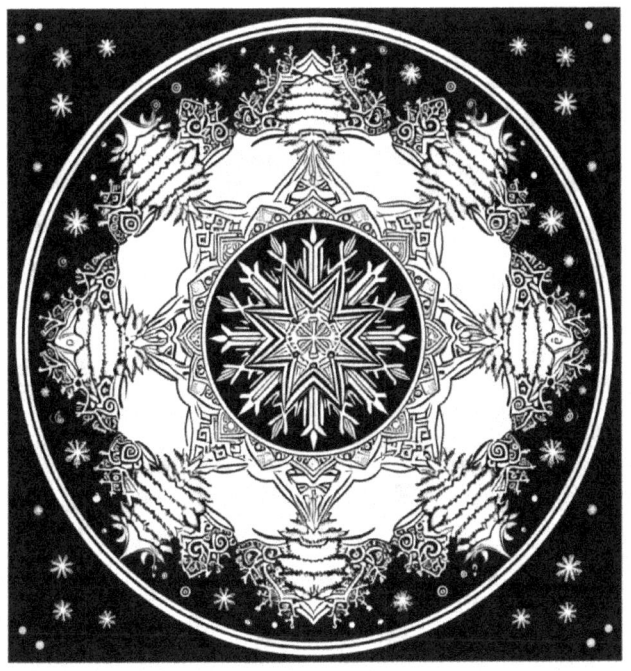

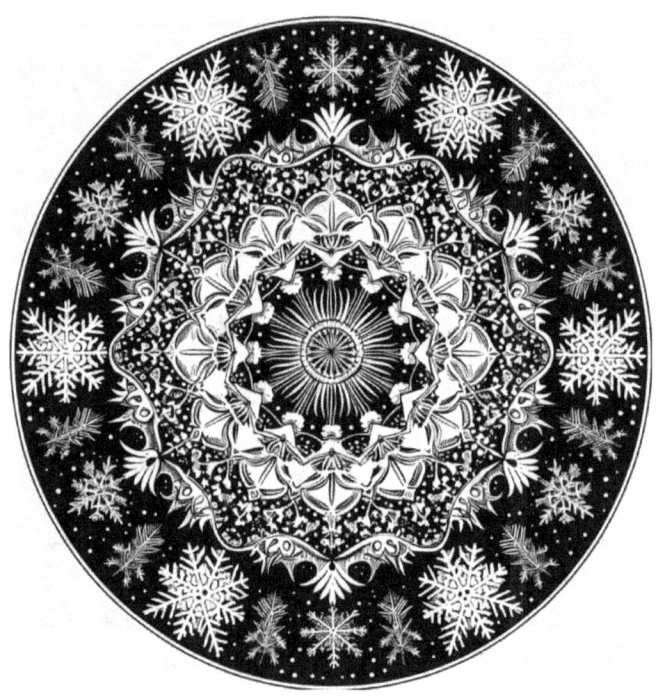

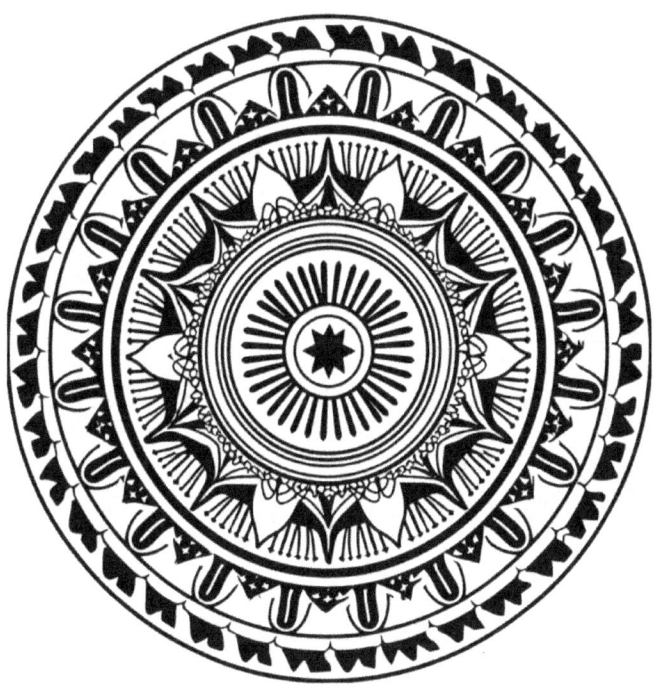

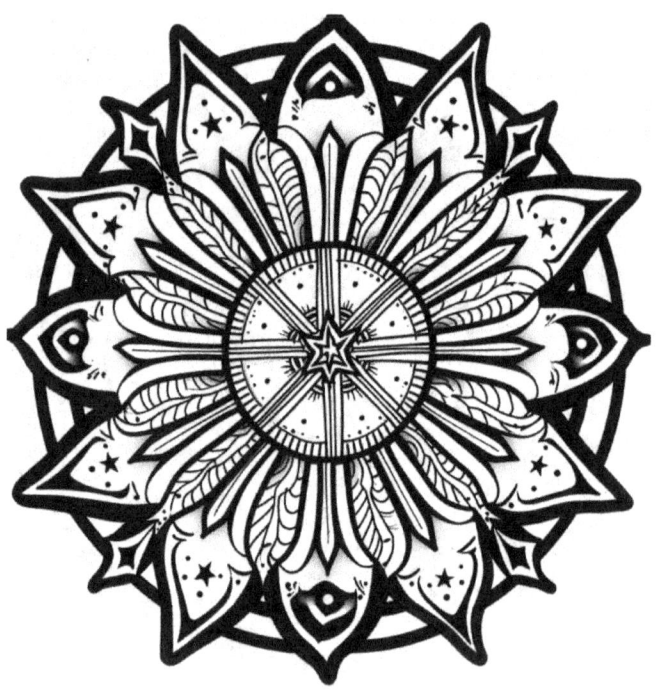

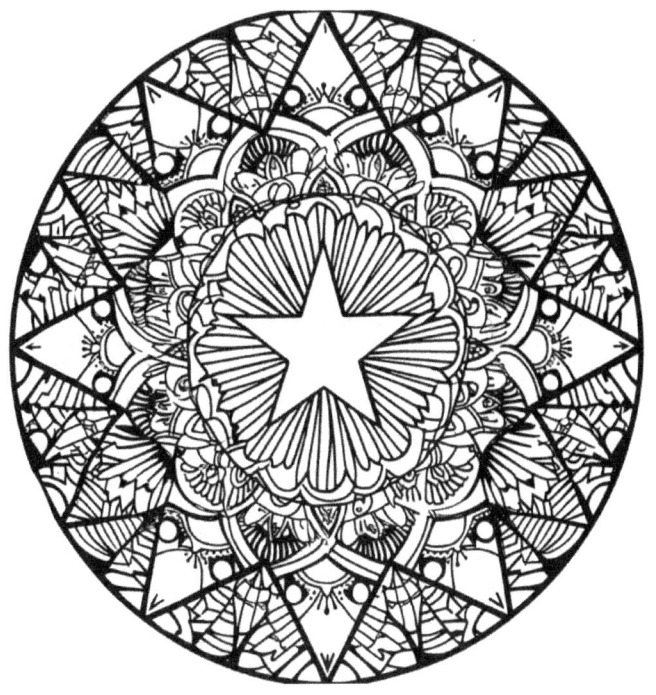

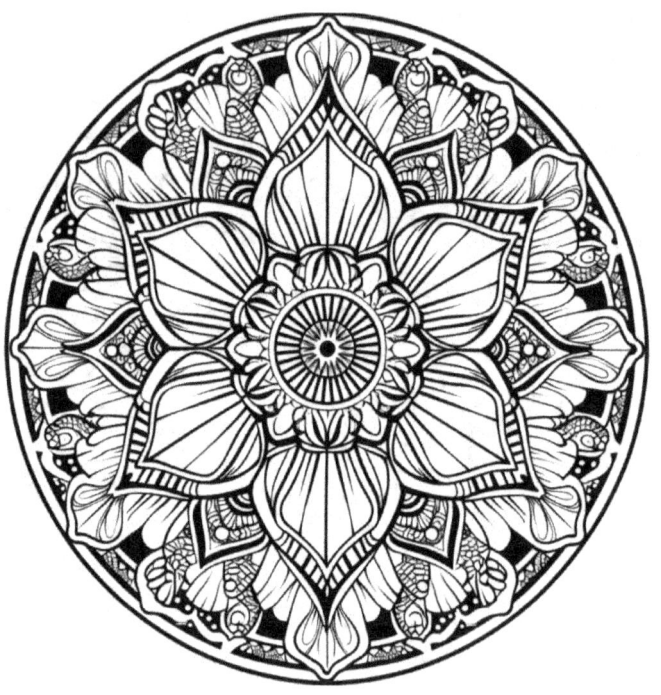

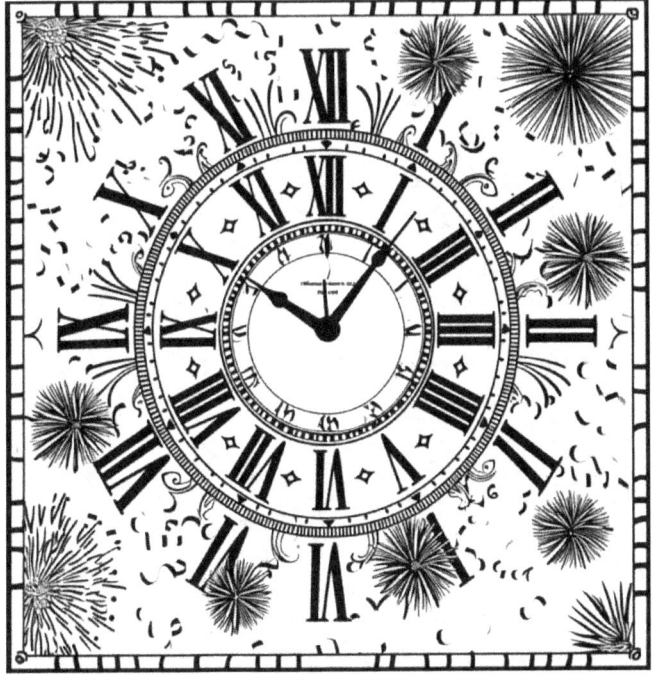

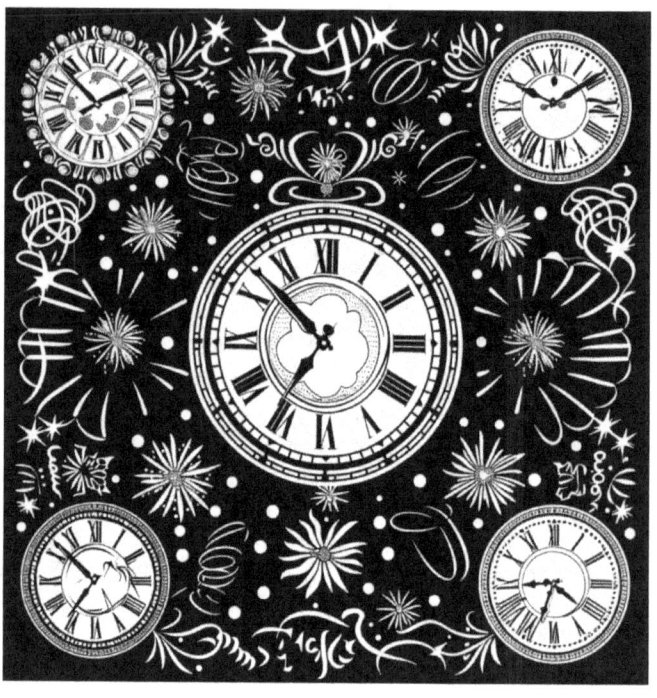

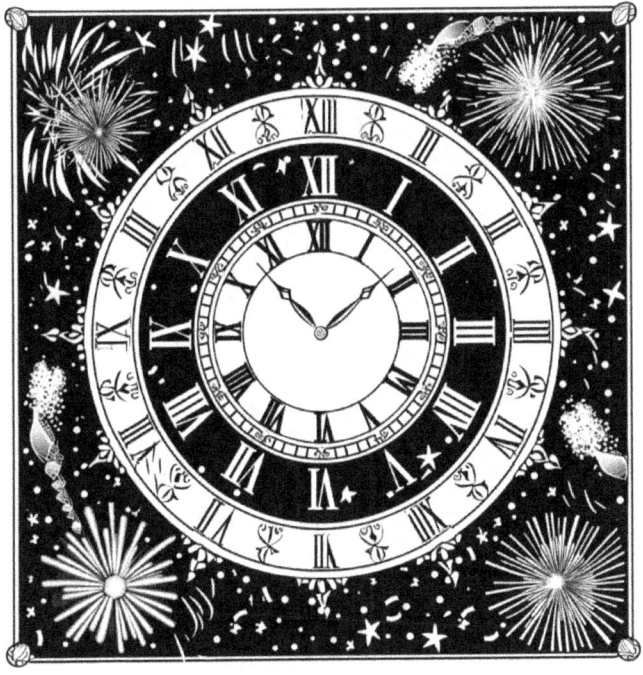

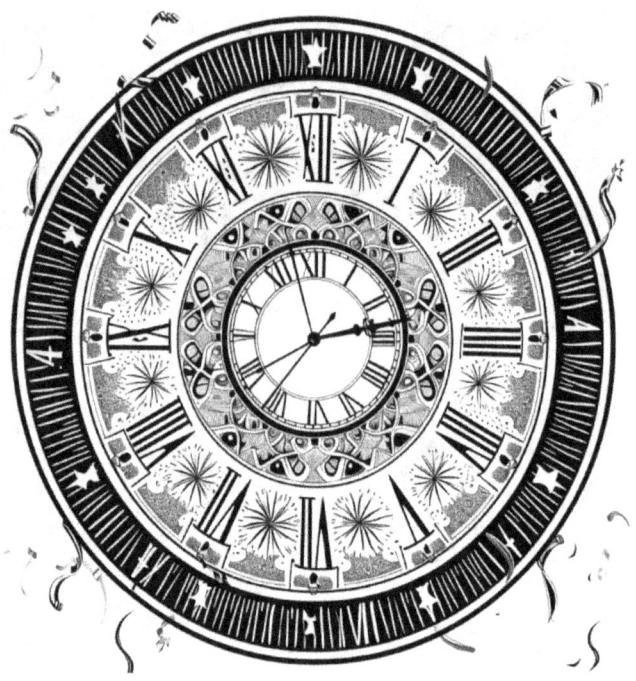

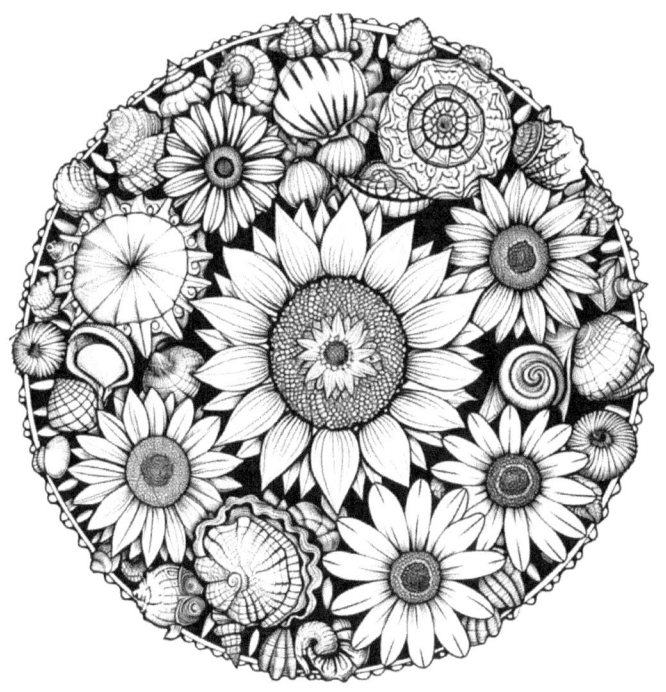

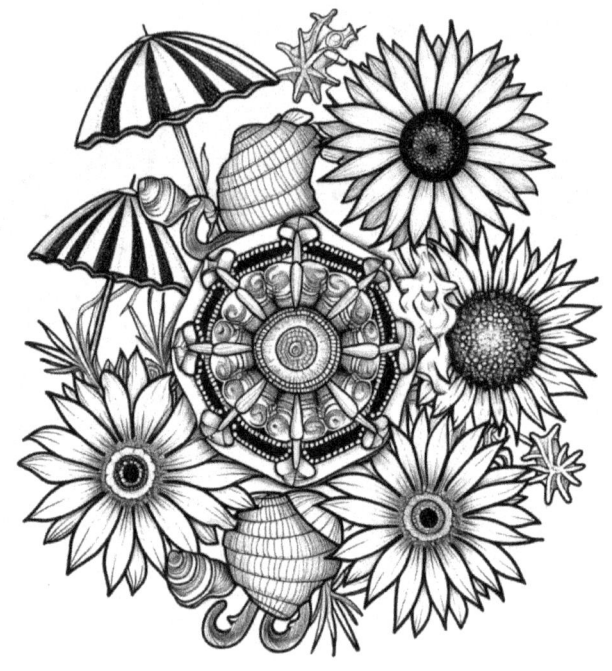

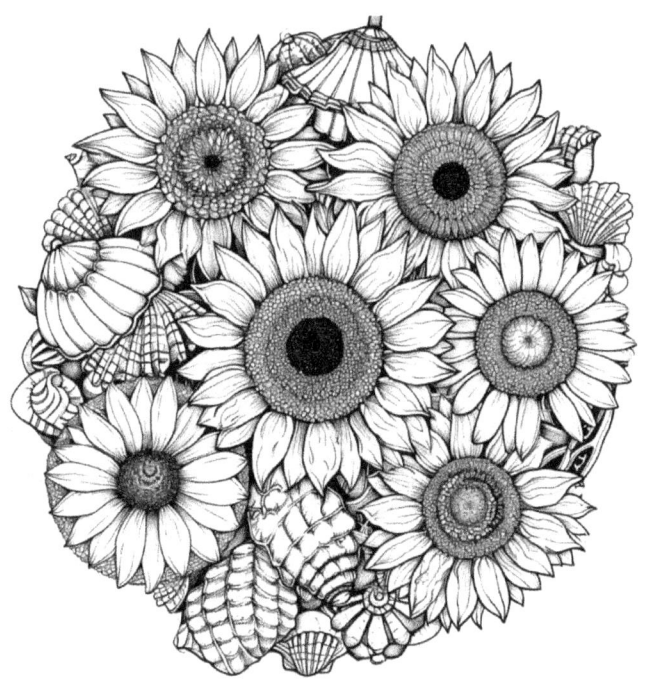

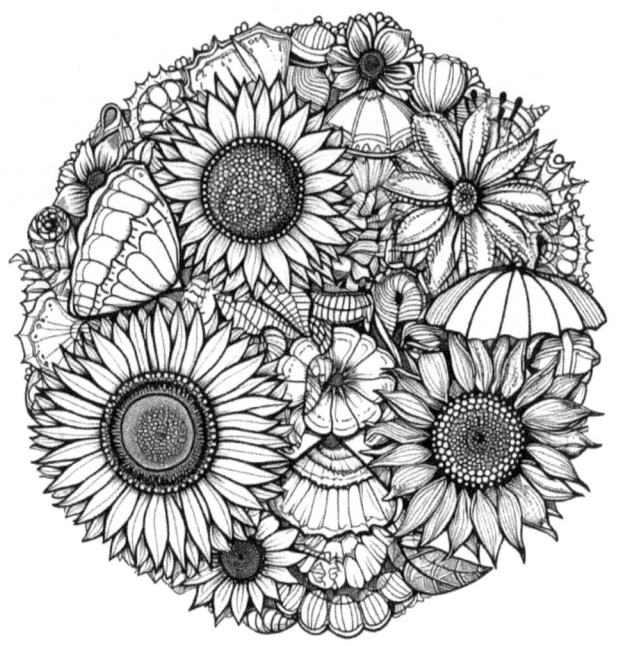

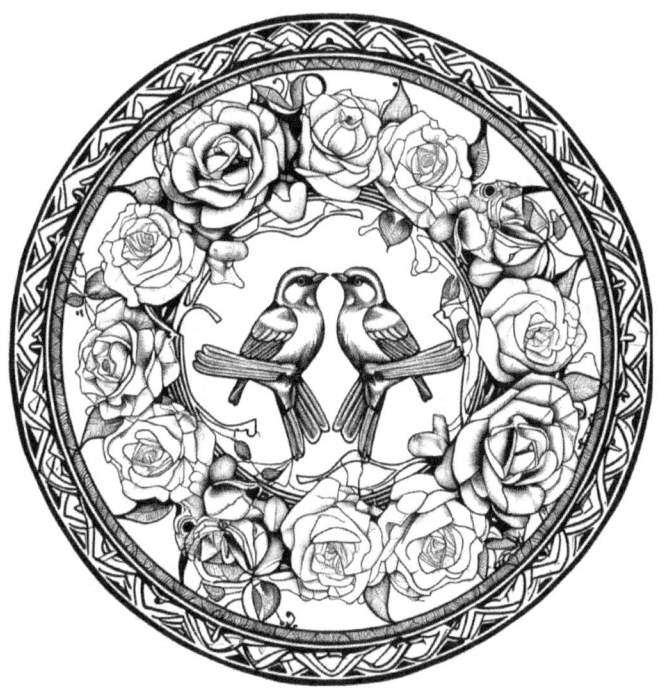

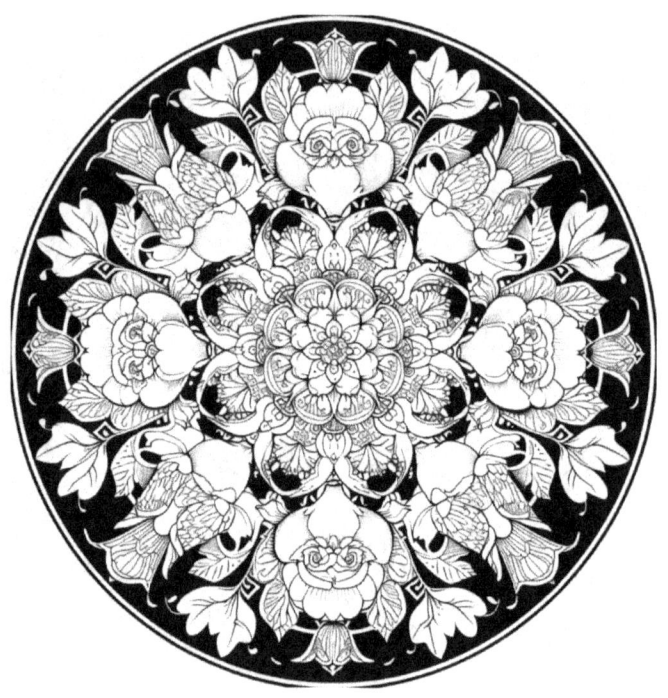

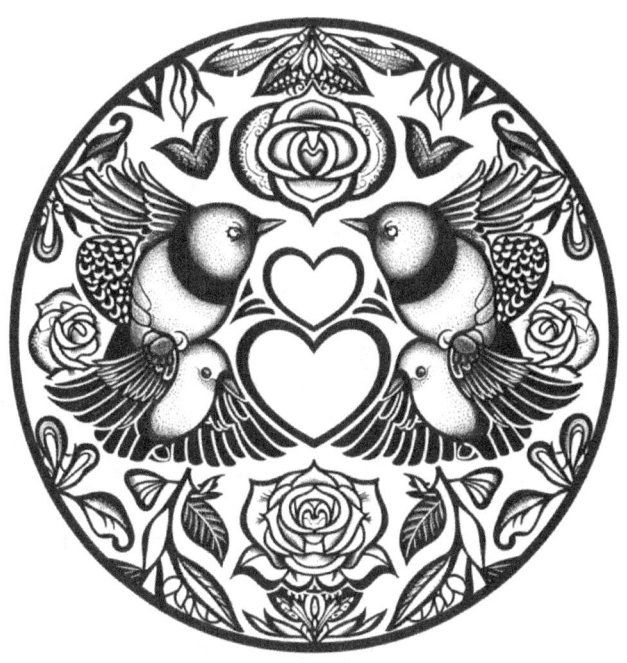

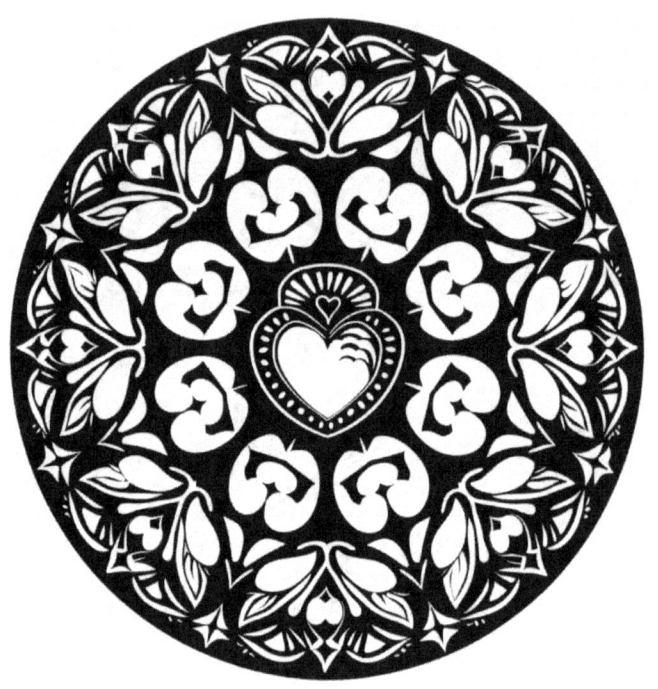

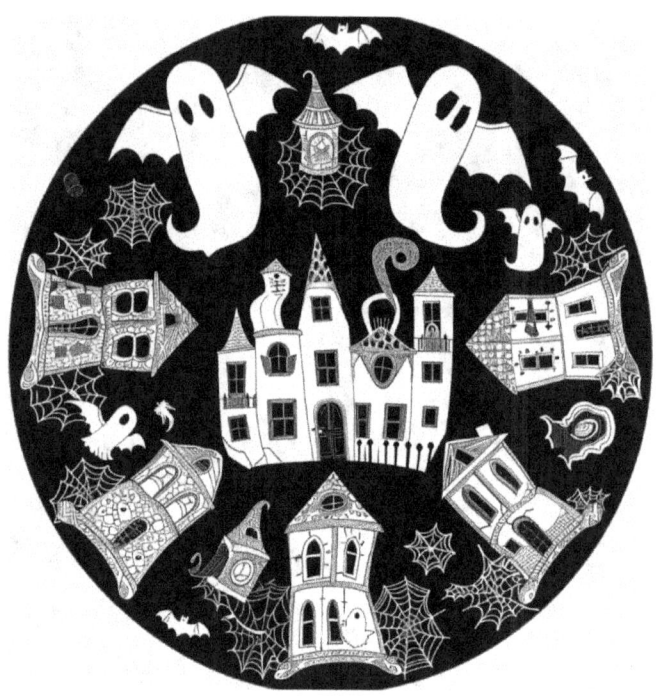

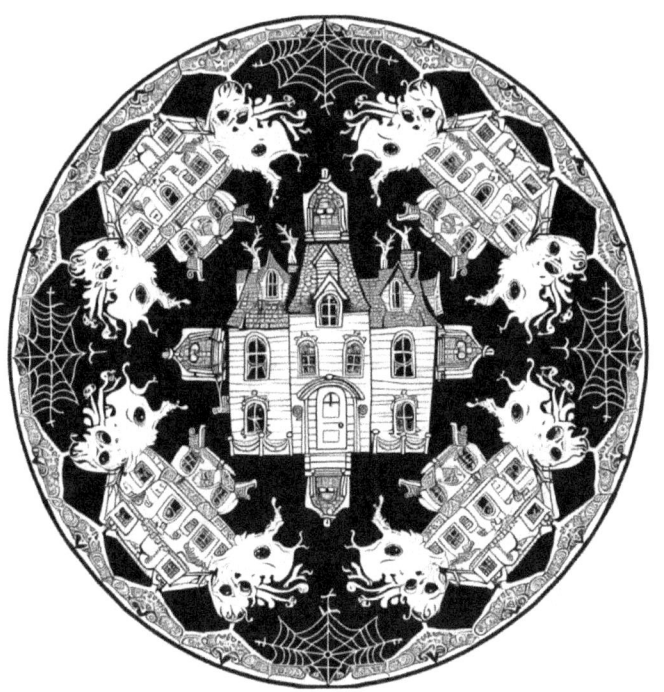

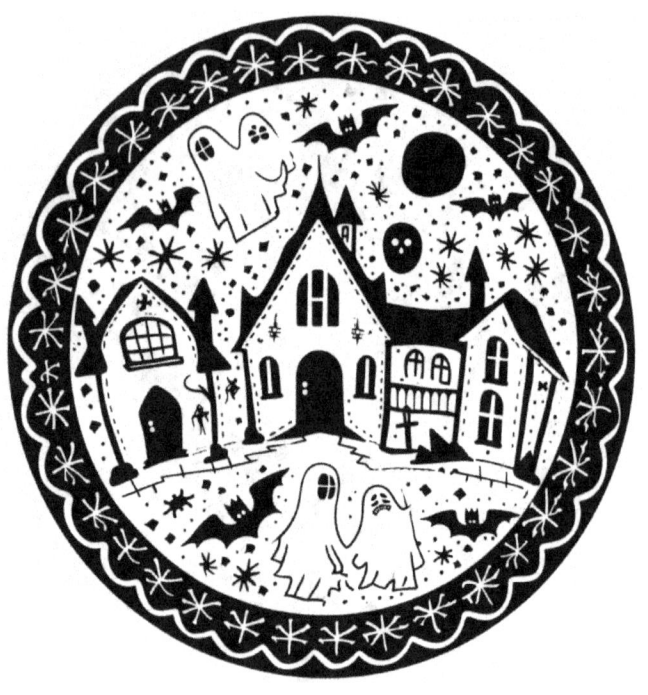

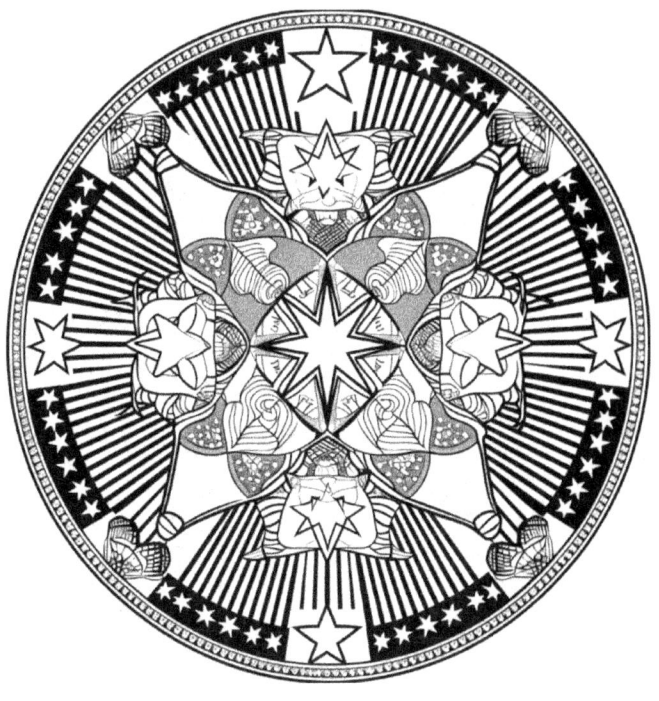

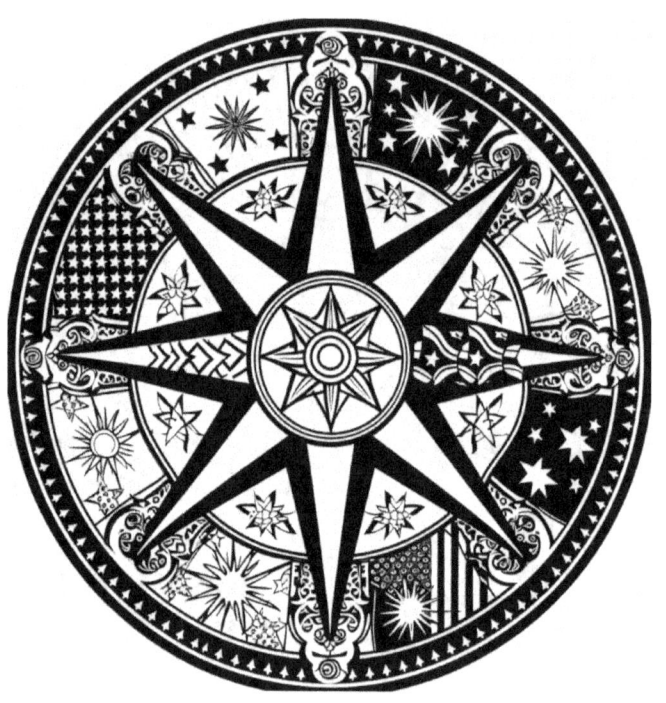

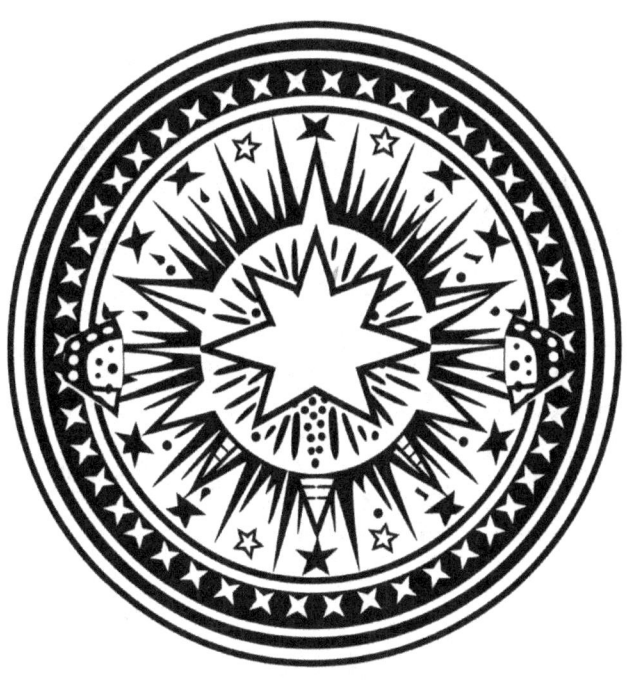

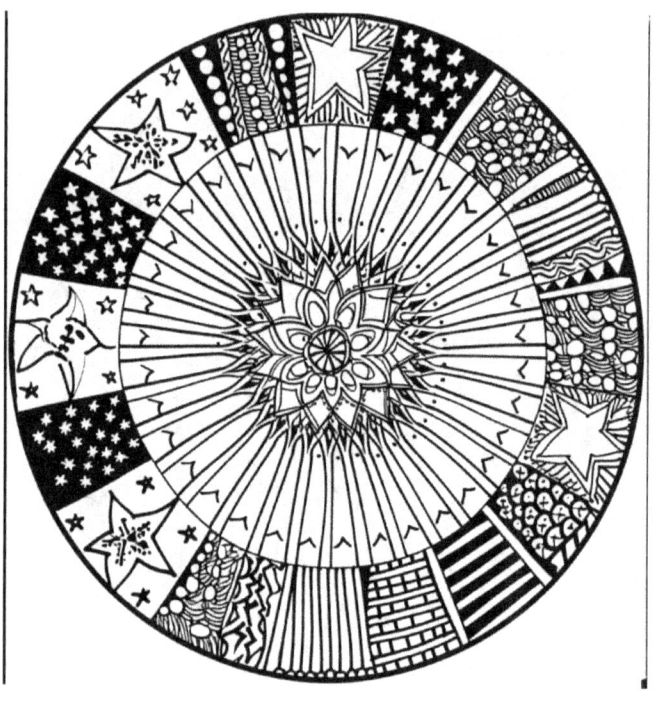

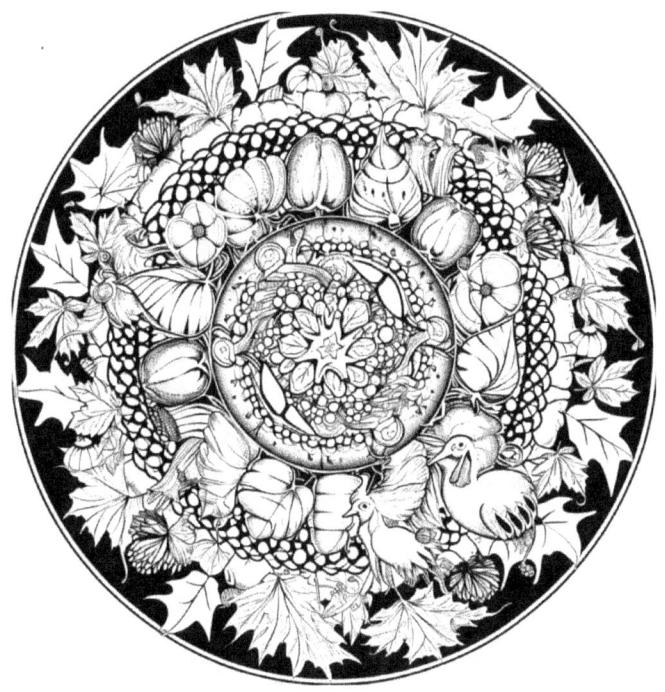

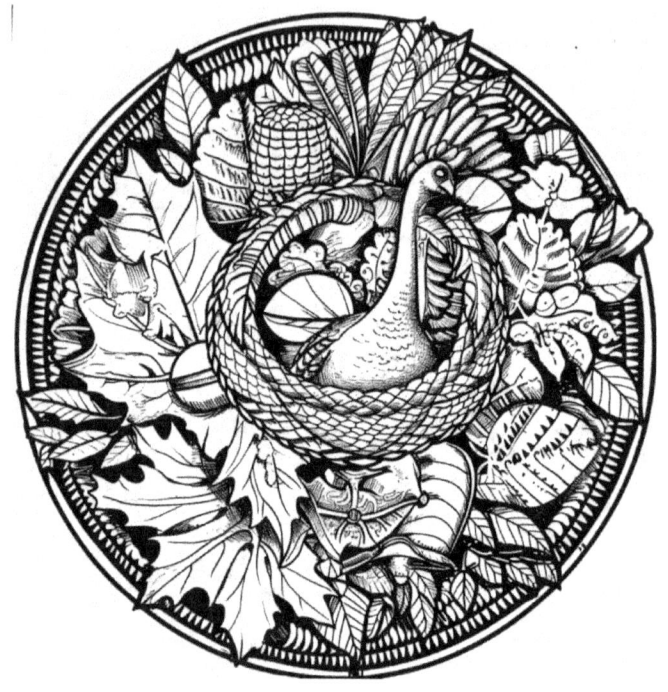

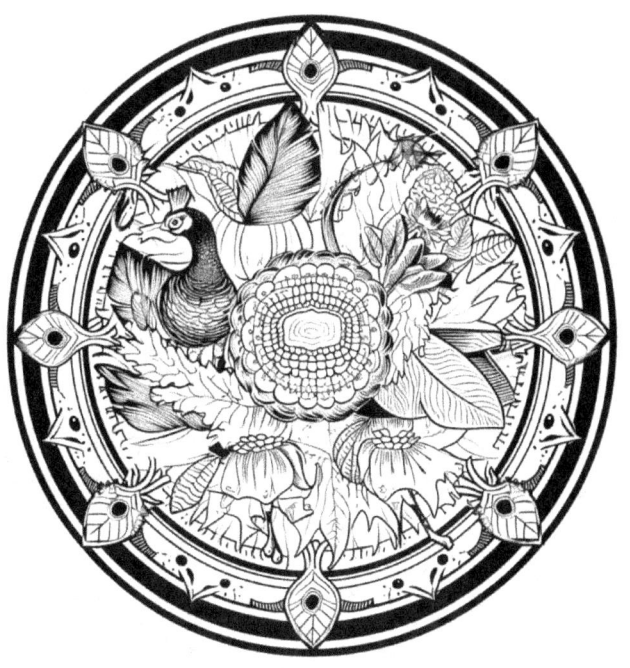

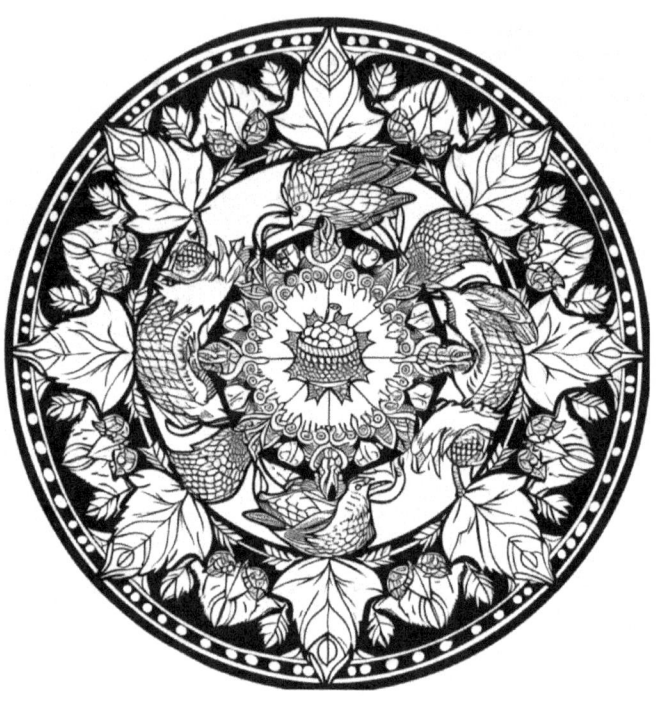

ABOUT THE AUTHOR

Lumina Visions is an artist who uses AI and new technologies to discover connections between art and Artificial Intelligence